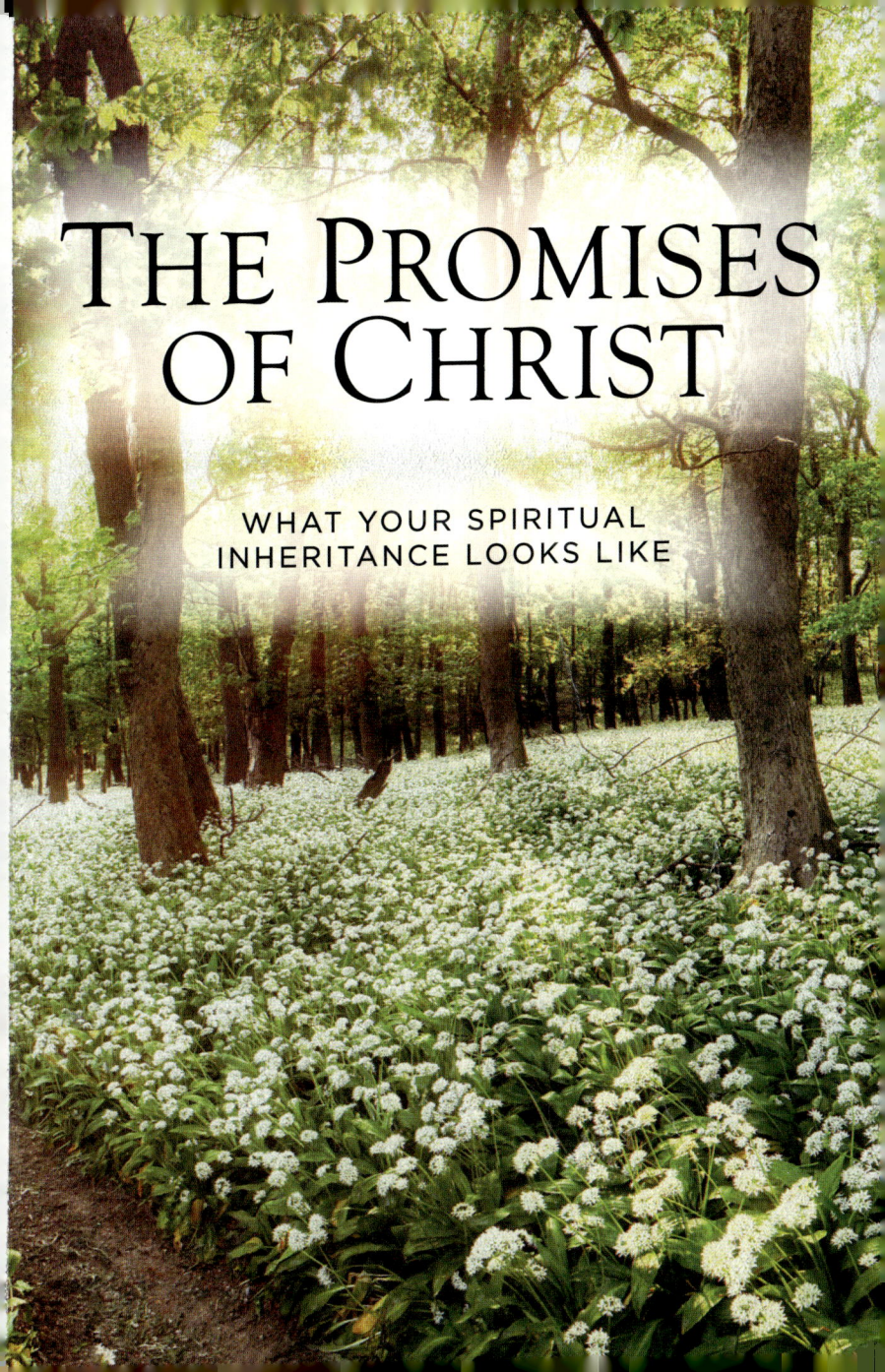

THE PROMISES OF CHRIST

WHAT YOUR SPIRITUAL
INHERITANCE LOOKS LIKE

The Promises of Christ: What Your Spiritual Inheritance Looks Like

Contents of this book include excerpts from *Knowing God as Father*, copyright © 1996 by James Robison; Published by LIFE Outreach International

Copyright© 2019 by Inprov, Ltd.
ISBN: 978-1-7327904-2-1

For further information, write Inprov, at:
2150 E. Continental Blvd, Southlake, TX 76092

All rights reserved. No part of this publication may be reproduced, stored in a retrieval system, or transmitted in any form or by any means, electronic, mechanical, photocopying, recording, or otherwise, without the prior written permission of the copyrights owners.

Scripture quotations marked (AMP) are taken from the Amplified® Bible, copyright © 1954, 1958, 1962, 1964, 1965, 1987 by The Lockman Foundation. Used by permission. www.Lockman.org

Scripture quotations marked (ESV) are from the ESV® Bible (The Holy Bible, English Standard Version®), copyright © 2001 by Crossway, a publishing ministry of Good News Publishers. Used by permission. All rights reserved.

Scripture quotations marked (MSG) are taken from THE MESSAGE, copyright © 1993, 1994, 1995, 1996, 2000, 2001, 2002 by Eugene H. Peterson. Used by permission of NavPress. All rights reserved. Represented by Tyndale House Publishers, Inc.

Scripture quotations marked (NASB) are taken from the New American Standard Bible®, copyright © 1960, 1962, 1963, 1968, 1971, 1972, 1973, 1975, 1977, 1995 by The Lockman Foundation. Used by permission. www.Lockman.org

Scripture quotations marked (NKJV) are taken from the New King James Version®. Copyright © 1982 by Thomas Nelson. Used by permission. All rights reserved.

Scripture quotations marked (NLT) are taken from the Holy Bible, New Living Translation, copyright ©1996, 2004, 2007, 2013, 2015 by Tyndale House Foundation. Used by permission of Tyndale House Publishers, Inc., Carol Stream, Illinois 60188. All rights reserved.

CONTENTS

INTRODUCTION

INSIGHT ONE: 6
Promises of His Word

INSIGHT TWO: 26
Hope in His Promises

INSIGHT THREE: 46
The Promise of Life

INSIGHT FOUR: 66
The Promise of the Prodigal

INSIGHT FIVE: 86
The Promise of Protection

INSIGHT SIX: 106
The Promise of Peace

INTRODUCTION

I've spent more than fifty years studying God's Word and sharing it with people all over the world. One of the most profound things I've discovered over these decades of study, growth and learning is that we have been given countless promises through God's Word.

God began promising things to mankind in the Old Testament, like when He promised that He would fight for us (Exodus 14:14). God promised things to us through His Son, Jesus Christ. Jesus promised that He would give us rest (Matthew 11:28). And our Heavenly Father has given us promises through the Holy Spirit, who works in us to finish the work He started (Philippians 1:6).

I pray that reading through this short selection of His many promises will help you come to realize how special our Father is. He truly loves us and wants the best for us, and we can absolutely believe His Word.

James Robison

James Robison

INSIGHT ONE:

Promises of His Word

The Bible is such an important tool for Christians. Filled with the Word of God, we have endless wisdom, love and grace right at our fingertips. All throughout Scripture, we find promises that God has given us, whether directly from Him to other believers, through Jesus Christ or through the writings of disciples and prophets.

Because God's Word is unfailing, we can stand on the promises He has left us with and know that they are true. A promise from God isn't like a promise from a friend or family member. As humans, sometimes we break promises or don't follow through. But we know that we can trust God and believe in His heavenly promises over our lives.

Throughout history, there have been pharaohs, emperors, presidents, prime ministers, kings and dictators who have promised to provide for our needs and oversee our lives. Too many times, the church has bought into that lie. We've actually handed off our responsibility to love our neighbors as ourselves. This must cease.

We have to return to His Word and the promises He has faithfully given us—the promises that are proven again and again each and every day through expressions of the Father's love. These are the promises that we know we can count on.

These promises are life-changing!

While it's tempting to trust in the promises of those in power, we must always return to our Heavenly King and His promises that will never fail.

Let us be reminded to spend time in His Word on a regular basis, not only to keep His promises fresh in our minds, but to continually draw closer to Him.

Let us call on these promises when storms pass through our lives and believe that joy will come in the morning. We will know the promise of His Spirit dwelling within us—that He said we wouldn't be alone, and we aren't!

As we navigate life, we can always turn to His Word and the many promises God has given us. He promises to be our strength, our protection, our foundation, our hope. When our flesh fails, He is there for us with an unfailing word and a strong right hand.

If we absolutely believe
every promise of God,
it would shift how we live.
But the problem is that we live
in a world that makes a lot of
promises and then doesn't deliver.
Like the diet where you lose
ten pounds by Tuesday,
tried it—didn't work!

— SHEILA WALSH

WORD OF ENCOURAGEMENT:

Jesus Christ is called "Emmanuel," which means, "God With Us." It was true when He walked the earth, and He promised it would be true forever. We need not miss Him. We just need to open our hearts and minds as we learn to **live in the light of His presence.**

— Randy Robison

WHATEVER GOD HAS PROMISED
GETS STAMPED WITH THE YES OF JESUS.
IN HIM, THIS IS WHAT WE PREACH AND
PRAY, THE GREAT AMEN, GOD'S YES AND
OUR YES TOGETHER, GLORIOUSLY EVIDENT.
GOD AFFIRMS US, MAKING US A SURE THING
IN CHRIST, PUTTING HIS YES WITHIN US.
BY HIS SPIRIT HE HAS STAMPED US WITH
HIS ETERNAL PLEDGE—A SURE BEGINNING
OF WHAT HE IS DESTINED TO COMPLETE.

2 Corinthians 1:20-22 (MSG)

GUEST: SHEILA WALSH

We need to get back to reading God's Word and knowing His promises. There are over 3,000 promises in God's Word! I found it interesting that the two words in the Old Testament that we translate as *promise* are "omer" and "dabar." They mean "to say" and "to speak." God didn't have to promise. All God had to do was to say or to speak.

We have so devalued the word *promise* that we have undervalued the power behind God's promises. When God makes a promise, we know that He will follow through and He will keep His word.

> "God is not a man that he should lie…"
> NUMBERS 23:19 (NKJV)

Excerpted from *LIFE TODAY* taping with Sheila Walsh, May 3, 2011.

For the word of God is living and active and sharper than any two-edged sword . . .

HEBREWS 4:12 (ESV)

PROMISE . . .

A heavenly promise from God is worth so much more than a human promise.

Just for God to speak, His Word can be counted as promise!

He does not lie; He does not fail. We can count on His promises and all the blessings they bring to our lives.

PRAYER:

Let us lean into Your promises today, Father. Where You have promised us peace, joy and contentment, let us believe and trust Your holy Word! Thank You for Your unfailing truths and for all the beauty they bring to our lives. Amen.

WORD OF ENCOURAGEMENT:

One of the most exciting promises Jesus left us with was that He would be back! In fact, in John 14:2–3 He promises that He will return for us. And from then on, we will be blessed to be with Him always. He's preparing a way for all of us, and we can have faith in His promise that

He is coming back!

"I GIVE THEM ETERNAL LIFE, AND THEY WILL NEVER PERISH, AND NO ONE WILL SNATCH THEM OUT OF MY HAND."

John 10:28 (ESV)

STORY: RANDY ROBISON

Imagine if you could have one magic verse that unlocked everything in life for you. Here's the one I would pick: *"If you ask Me anything in My name, I will do it"* (John 14:14, ESV).

Wouldn't that be great? Just name it, tag Jesus' name onto it, and *poof!*, there it is. For years, I thought that it was generally supposed to work that way. When it didn't, I figured that I was either not "in Jesus' name," whatever that meant, or that I had just asked "amiss," as James alluded to in his epistle (see James 4:3). Of course, both were probably true in many cases, but I also know that there were times when I asked for something not for myself when I was fully abiding in Christ, like when my younger sister was battling cancer. Still, she died.

So what is going on with that promise? We asked and God didn't do it, or so it seemed. When we look at the context of that statement, we find Jesus proclaiming to His disciples that He and the Father are one. He then tells them, *"Whatever you ask in My name, that will I do, so that the Father may be glorified in the Son. If you ask Me anything in My name, I will do it"* (John 14:13–14, NASB).

In order to understand it, I had to go back to the eight Greek words that make up verse 13: *hos aiteo onoma poieo hina pater doxazo huios.* It could be rendered, *Whatever is needed for those under my authority, I will provide in order that the Father can magnify the Son.*

Those who ask are not the focal point of the statement. In fact, the Greek word for "you" (*su*) is not there, nor is it in similar statements in Matthew 7:7 and 21:22. It's not "whatever you ask for, you get." The key is the conjunction "*in order that.*" Whatever is asked under Christ's authority, He will provide in order that He is glorified. We ask, and He provides in such a way that He receives the glory.

That changes everything. And that's precisely what our family saw through the sorrow of losing my sister. God was glorified—even in her pain and in her passing.

So learn His voice, hear it and ask away.

Don't be afraid to ask.

Our loving Father isn't anxious for the opportunity to condemn us or prove our lack of faith—remember, He only asked for faith the size of a mustard seed. Just know that His promised answer will always come in a way that glorifies Him. In that, we can all rejoice.

VICTORY . . .

In Christ, we have already won. We are victors. Death has been defeated, Jesus rose again and we have been given the promise of eternal life—the promise of victory!

And this is the promise that He has promised us—eternal life (1 John 2:25, NKJV).

PRAYER:

Father, we pray to be fearless in asking! We know that through You, all things can be accomplished. But we pray that what we ask for glorifies You. We trust in Your promised answer to us, and we rejoice in Your blessings over us. Amen.

WORD OF ENCOURAGEMENT:

It's amazing how easy it can be to forget all that God freely gives us.

The biggest gift of all—His Son on the cross

meant that our sins are forgiven, and we are promised an eternity with Him in heaven. God, help us not to forget Your promises. Let us cling to them and remember how precious they are. We have been given the greatest gift that anyone could ever give, and we are so grateful!

THE LORD KEPT HIS WORD AND DID FOR SARAH EXACTLY WHAT HE HAD PROMISED.

Genesis 21:1 (NLT)

Without a proper
relationship with God,
every one of us is doomed,
not only to continue
behavior that keeps us
in a pit of despair and defeat,
but also to be eternally
cut off from the very life
God so freely offers.

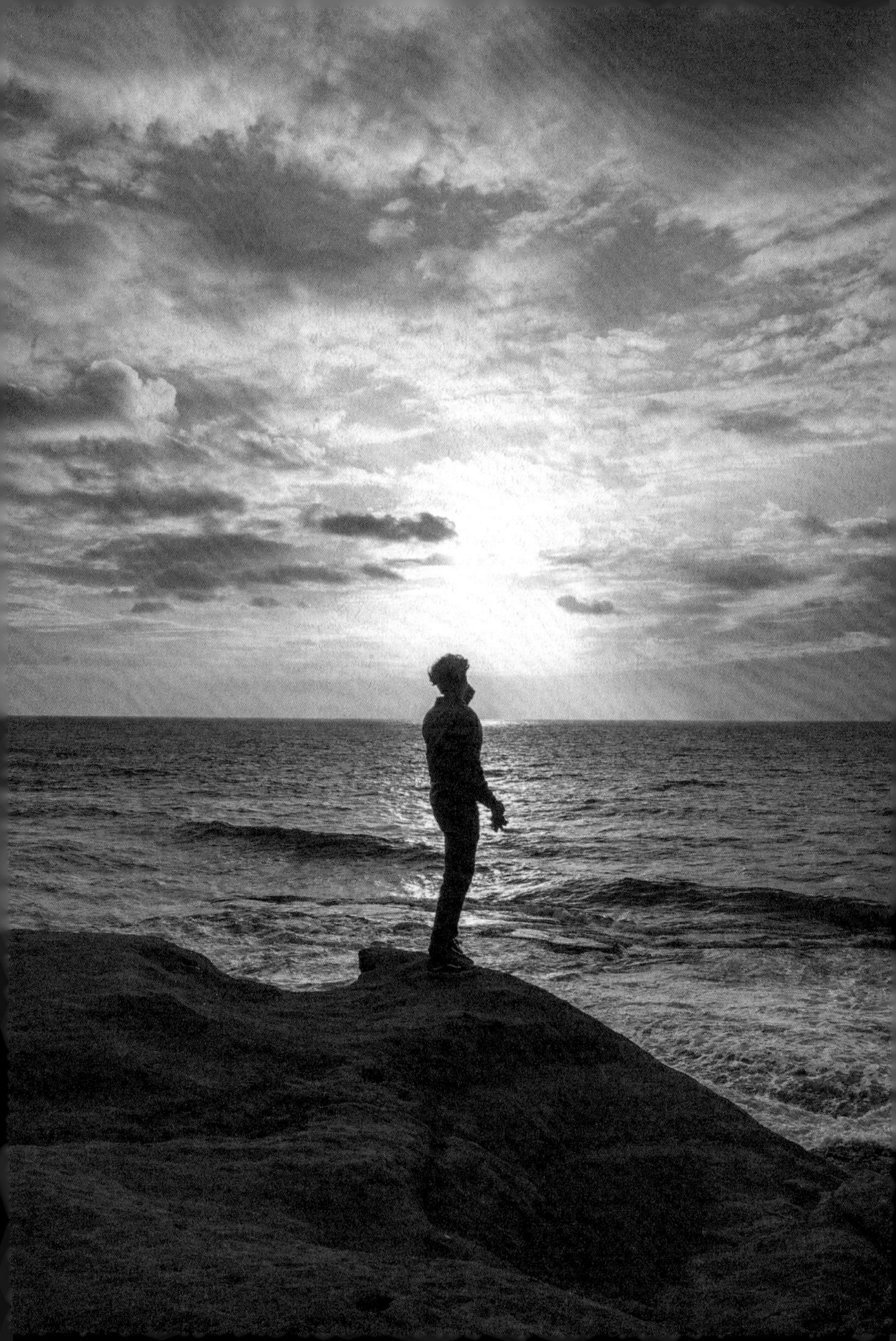

INSIGHT TWO:

Hope in His Promises

One of the biggest blessings we gain from the promises of Christ is the gift of hope! Not only do we have hope because of the promises God has made to us, but we can also cling to Him as our hope.

We learn a lot about His promises of hope throughout Scripture as we see illustrations of people who were utterly hopeless, and then found hope to cling to when they turned to God. In a world that so often brings us trials, challenges and unsteady circumstances, having hope can be such a lifesaver.

God is the One to cling to, our source of joy and protection in the midst of darkness.

Christ offered endless hope as He walked the earth. He healed the sick, He welcomed the outcasts of society, He forgave all sins, He performed miracles and brought freedom.

Wherever Jesus went, hope went, too. His hope is still with us today. Though He doesn't physically walk the earth anymore, He still invites us to become a part of His family. He forgives us when we mess up, comforts us when we are lonely, heals us when we are hurting, loves us—even when we don't feel loveable—and miracles are still happening before our very eyes.

There are times when we may not *feel* His presence and circumstances may cause us to be discouraged. That is when we can pray Romans 15:13 over ourselves: *May the God of hope fill you with all joy and peace as you trust in him, so that you may overflow with hope by the power of the Holy Spirit* (NIV). As we

rest in His promises and cling to Him as our hope,

let the redemption that comes as a result wash over us. And let us become extensions of that hope to others who may be feeling alone in a dark place.

Daniel walked into the lions' den
with all the odds against him.
Not only was he thrown into a den
of lions, but the lions were ravenous.
Everything indicated that Daniel
would not walk out of the den alive;
however, Daniel had hope!
He remained steadfast in his faith
that God would protect him
and see him through. And in the end,
Daniel's faith brought glory to God.

WORD OF ENCOURAGEMENT:

When the Israelites doubted God, and as a result wandered the desert for 40 years, there may have been days when there was little hope. Yet, God stayed true to His promises. He provided them with manna and sustenance, and He followed through on the promise of the Promised Land. Even when we fail, **God's promises are still available to us.**

THIS HOPE WE HAVE AS AN ANCHOR OF THE SOUL, A HOPE BOTH SURE AND STEADFAST AND ONE WHICH ENTERS WITHIN THE VEIL.

Hebrews 6:19 (NASB)

GUEST: HOLLY WAGNER

Jesus told us that in this world we would have tough times, but in the next breath, He promised that we should be of good cheer because He has overcome the world. Yes, you will encounter storms, but you can have hope because He will see you through!

I have heard that people can live about forty days without food, three days without water, and eight minutes without air. But they can live only one second without hope. Hope is more than optimism. In the New Testament, the biblical definition of hope implies a knowing, a sure expectation.

When hopelessness fills your heart, death begins to take over—death to your dreams, to a relationship worth saving, to the idea that things will get better. The power of hope coursing through your veins can be your most valuable asset because it creates a tremendous force within you.

> Hope is not a luxury; it is an essential.

Hope can change tragedy to opportunity, dreaded work to exciting, worthwhile effort, and weariness to invincibility.

Hope is for all of us. Not just those "glass half full" people. Hope is not wishing; it is not positive thinking. It is a sure expectation that God will do what He promised. Hope is like floaties. Have you seen children in a pool wearing those little floatation armbands in order to keep their heads above water? Hope is like that. It keeps you floating until you get to solid ground.

Sometimes the bravest thing you can do is to keep hoping; and oftentimes, to keep a grip on hope will take both hands. Where are you drowning? Put on those floaties. You are being made stronger with every wave, and this storm is not bigger than the God who dwells in you. His name is Immanuel—"God With Us."

Excerpted from Find Your Brave *by Holly Wagner, Copyright © 2016 by Holly Wagner. Excerpted by permission of WaterBrook, a division of Penguin Random House, LLC.*

HOPE...

In Jeremiah 29:11, God tells us that He has plans for us. Plans for good, not evil, plans for prosperity and hope! The Creator of the Universe has plans for each and every human on earth and has hope for all of us. What a beautiful gift. We know from Romans that we can *abound in hope by the power of the Holy Spirit* (Romans 15:13, NASB). Hope overflowing!

PRAYER:

God, let us not forget how essential hope is. When we let Your holy hope into our hearts, we are emboldened, encouraged and empowered. Your hope can course through our veins and give us a sure expectation of what is to come. We are so grateful for this promise of hope! Amen.

WORD OF ENCOURAGEMENT:

Christ in you is the hope of glory (see Colossians 1:27). When we accept Christ into our hearts, we automatically have a hope that is supernatural. ## We have hope in an eternity with God, hope that our sins have been forgiven and a hope that we can share with others—both those already in the body of Christ and those who do not yet have this intrinsic hope.

WE PUT OUR HOPE IN THE LORD.
HE IS OUR HELP AND OUR SHIELD.

Psalm 33:20 (NLT)

STORY: REBEKAH LYONS

The life of the believer hangs in the balance between the now and the not yet. We know the hope—that the kingdom would come on earth as it is in heaven—but we live in the waiting. In the same way, we can know the call of God on our lives and feel anxious to get to it, but sometimes God calls us to wait as he refines us, as he shows himself to be our redeemer, rescuer, and healer. We must confess that his timing is best, and trust and declare that the waiting will bring us into a place of readiness. Perhaps you are waiting in hope that a broken relationship will be repaired. Maybe you are waiting for the return of a loved one with whom you've lost touch. Perhaps you've held off on divorce, hoping for the restoration of your marriage. Maybe you're waiting for physical healing.

You straddle promise and doubt, feebly holding on to the hope of promise. Keep holding on. You may not know the outcome, but you can rest in the tension of the waiting. It's in the tension that the music is made. Remember the song of the psalmist, "How long, Lord?"

When will you show up in all your glory and

swoop the brokenhearted into your palm? When will you fly by and tuck us in your mighty wings? We sit on the precipice of promise, and the posture of waiting requires ultimate surrender of the human will. No matter how much we want to change things or rush them, we cannot. It is out of our hands.

Here, in the waiting, God gently responds . . .

There will come a moment in your waiting when God says, "It's time." There is a season for each of us, where we will reap if we do not faint. He shows us the way. We need grace and wisdom to sit in the places prepared for us, because we've been given an anointing to be revealed in time. God has something in store for you and only you. Waiting is a critical part of your anointing. It prepares you, strengthens you, equips and trains you to step up when the moment comes.

Excerpted from You Are Free: Be Who You Already Are *by Rebekah Lyons. Copyright ©2017 by Rebekah Lyons. Published by Zondervan. Used by permission.*

COURAGE...

Having and maintaining hope and faith when circumstances are difficult to navigate can be a real challenge. Scripture tells us we can have courage because of Christ—He is with us, our source of hope and a presence of sanctity. Allow His Spirit to encourage you that you may maintain your hope and faith in Him, no matter what you may be facing!

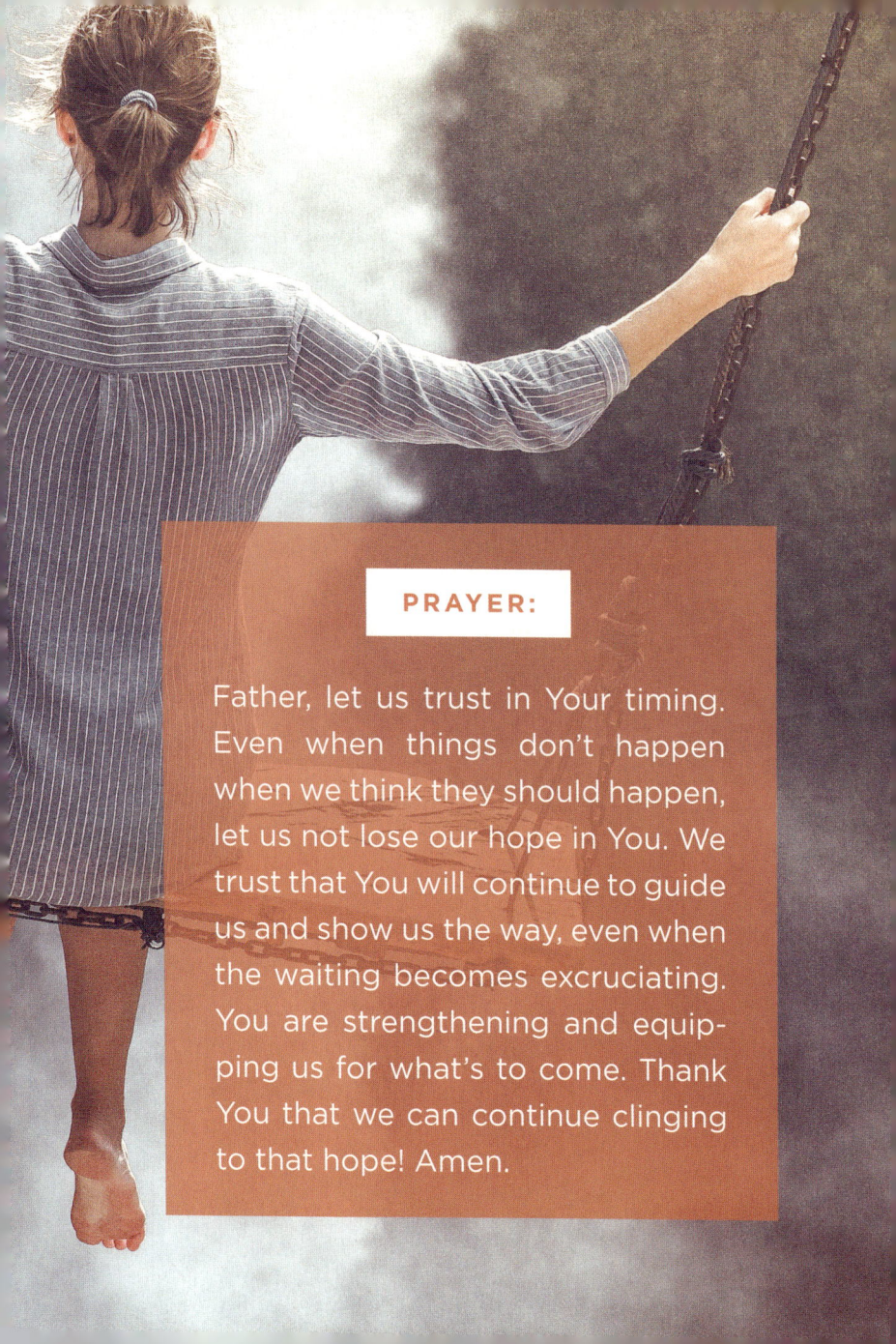

PRAYER:

Father, let us trust in Your timing. Even when things don't happen when we think they should happen, let us not lose our hope in You. We trust that You will continue to guide us and show us the way, even when the waiting becomes excruciating. You are strengthening and equipping us for what's to come. Thank You that we can continue clinging to that hope! Amen.

WORD OF ENCOURAGEMENT:

One day children were brought to Jesus in the hope that he would lay hands on them and pray over them. The disciples shooed them off. But Jesus intervened: "Let the children alone, don't prevent them from coming to me. God's kingdom is made up of people like these." After laying hands on them, he left (Matthew 19:13–15, MSG).

When we have hope in Christ, He delights in that hope. We can approach Him at any time with hope in our hearts and know that **He welcomes us.**

THROUGH THE LORD'S MERCIES
WE ARE NOT CONSUMED,
BECAUSE HIS COMPASSIONS FAIL NOT.
THEY ARE NEW EVERY MORNING;
GREAT IS YOUR FAITHFULNESS.
"THE LORD IS MY PORTION," SAYS MY SOUL,
"THEREFORE I HOPE IN HIM!"

Lamentations 3:22–24 (NKJV)

I suspect you would never intend this, but this is what happens: When you attempt to live by your own religious plans and projects, you are cut off from Christ, you fall out of grace. Meanwhile, we expectantly wait for a satisfying relationship with the Spirit. For in Christ, neither our most conscientious religion nor disregard of religion amounts to anything. What matters is something far more interior: faith expressed in love.

GALATIANS 5:4-6 (MSG)

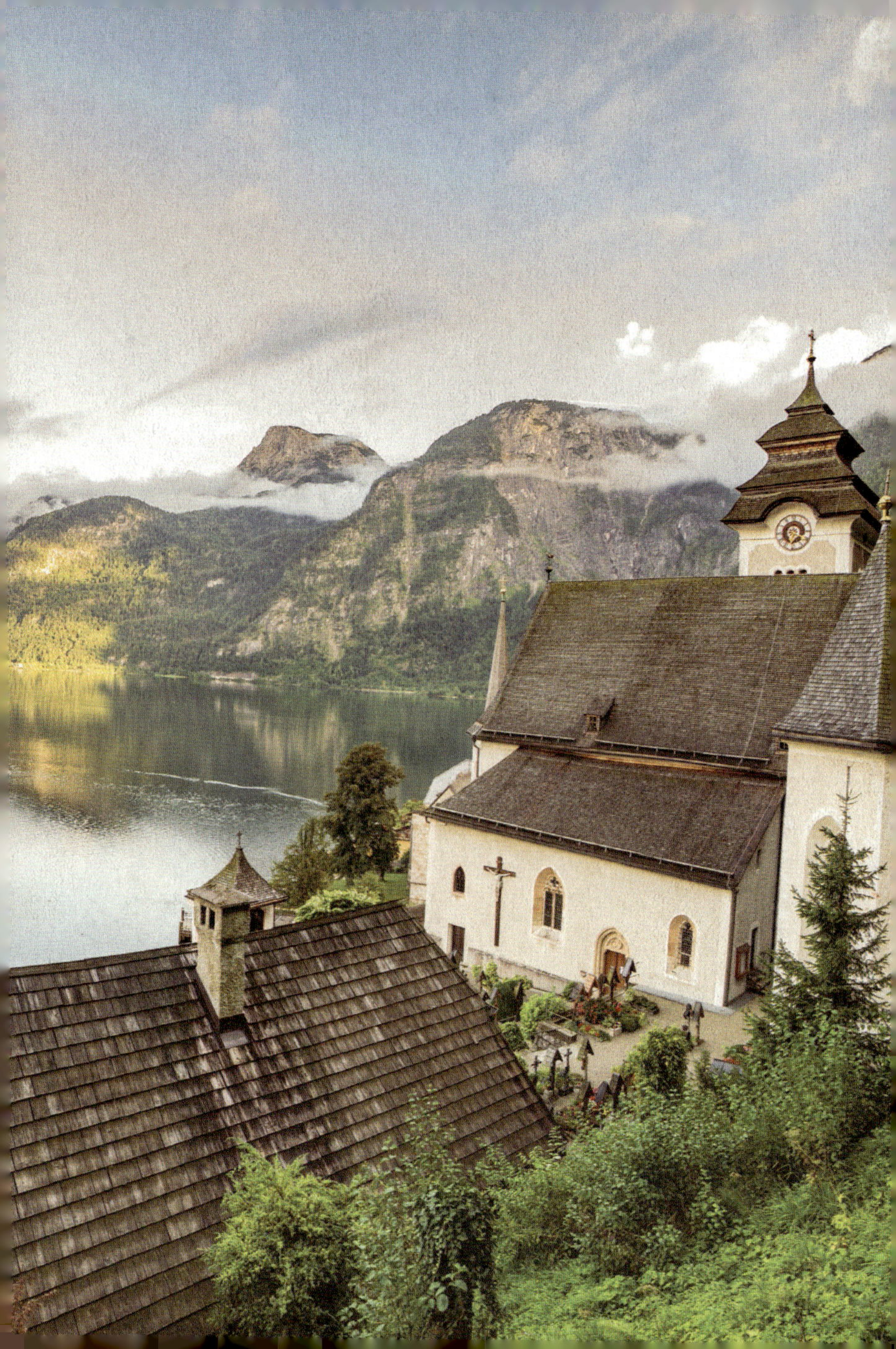

INSIGHT THREE:

The Promise of Life

It is impossible with human wisdom to understand how God took away that old sin nature and gave us His divine nature. But He did so by making us one with Jesus Christ when He was crucified. He placed your sin nature in Him; and when He died, that "Old Man" died with Him. It was buried with Him. Then, when He was raised, you were raised with Him to share His new resurrection life.

We have been promised that in Christ, we are new creations. The old has gone and the new has come. What a blessing to be given the promise of new life. And not only new life, but a new life that is blessed with the provision, protection, wisdom and love of our Heavenly Father.

We are no longer slaves to sin.

We can now yield our lives to God as His instruments. And, though we may sin from time to time, we don't have to let any sin dominate our lives. Under grace, we have a new nature. And sin no longer rules over us because in this new nature, we have God working in and through us to deliver us from the power of sin.

What an amazing promise we have been given—the promise of a new nature in Christ, one in which we are covered by His abounding grace. Even when we fail and fall short, we don't lose our reward in this new life we have been given.

And not only have we been given a new life and a new nature through Christ, but in Christ we are also promised the gift of eternity. Our life extends into His Kingdom once we have been saved, and we know this because God sent Jesus Christ to die for our sins that we may have the gift of eternal life (see John 3:16).

I am so amazed by the promises God has given to us about our lives on earth and the eternal life we will one day walk into. To even have life is such an incredible gift, but how much richer it becomes when we invite Jesus into our hearts and live it out with Him!

*My old self has been
crucified with Christ.
It is no longer I who live,
but Christ lives in me.
So I live in this earthly body
by trusting in the Son of God,
who loved me and
gave himself for me.*

GALATIANS 2:20 (NLT)

What a beautiful promise
of life and sacrifice that we have
been given. Thank You, Jesus,
for the life You've given us!

WORD OF ENCOURAGEMENT:

According to the Bible you are good simply because God made you in his image. Period. He cherishes you because you bear a resemblance to him. And you will only be satisfied when you engage in your role as an image bearer of God. Such was the view of King David: *"As for me, I will see Your face in righteousness; I shall be satisfied when I awake in Your likeness"* (Psalm 17:15, NKJV). Lay hold of this promise and spare yourself a world of confusion and fear. How much sadness would evaporate if every person simply chose to believe this:

I was made for God's glory and am being made into his image.

Excerpted from Unshakable Hope: Building Our Lives on the Promises of God *by Max Lucado. Copyright © 2018 by Max Lucado. Used by permission of Thomas Nelson.*

LET US SEIZE AND HOLD TIGHTLY THE CONFESSION OF OUR HOPE WITHOUT WAVERING, FOR HE WHO PROMISED IS RELIABLE AND TRUSTWORTHY AND FAITHFUL [TO HIS WORD].

Hebrews 10:23 (AMP)

> **GUEST: ROBERT MORRIS**

When Jesus Christ walked the earth, He often removed himself from the crowds. We're familiar with the time He miraculously fed five thousand families, but we don't usually remember the context. Just before that day, Jesus' beloved cousin John (called "John the Baptist") was beheaded by King Herod.

Jesus withdrew to a secluded place, but people discovered where He was and a huge crowd sought Him out. That's why there were so many people in a remote place with no food.

Jesus felt compassion toward them and healed the sick.

As the hour became late, they grew hungry, prompting the dinner miracle. After they had all eaten, Jesus sent the crowds home and even sent His disciples on their way.

Matthew's gospel tells us, *Immediately He made the disciples get into the boat and go ahead of Him to the other side, while He sent the crowds away. After He had sent the crowds away, He went up on the mountain by Himself to pray; and when it was evening, He was there alone* (Matthew 14:22–23, NASB).

Let us not neglect time for rest and prayer and time with Him. These quiet times refresh our hearts and minds and bring lightness to our life. It is so important to guard our schedules. When we make rest a priority, taking time to breathe in, be still and know that He is God, it makes a world of difference.

Excerpted from LIFE Today *taping with Robert Morris. 6/24/18.*

NEW...

God makes all things new. In Christ, we are given new life. He renews our spirits, our hope, our minds. He brings newness to our outlook and attitude. With Christ in our hearts, our old selves are gone, and we become new through Him!

PRAYER:

Father, You've given us the gift of life with You! Help us to live it out in the best way that we can, trusting in Your promises and provision. You bring so much goodness and enrich us with Your wisdom, grace and mercy. Help us remember that You are with us every moment, guiding us and leading us in Your ways. Amen.

WORD OF ENCOURAGEMENT:

I wonder how many people—even Christians—fully realize that their real life comes from God. I am talking about eternal life. Life that never ends. Life that can be experienced right now in all its fullness and abundance by everyone who has been born from above. In Him, we live and move and have our existence, the Bible says in Acts 17:28. Apart from Him, we would not have life—because there is no life apart from Him. In Ephesians 2:1, we are told that we are dead in our sins before we receive Jesus as Savior. We were dead spiritually. But our Heavenly Father has brought us to life spiritually. And spiritual life is what really counts. Physical life always ends in death, but **spiritual life goes on forever.**

GOD IS NOT A MAN, SO HE DOES NOT LIE. HE IS NOT HUMAN, SO HE DOES NOT CHANGE HIS MIND. HAS HE EVER SPOKEN AND FAILED TO ACT? HAS HE EVER PROMISED AND NOT CARRIED IT THROUGH?

Numbers 23:19 (NLT)

STORY: LISA BEVERE

As God puts His hand on us, it is evidenced in our lives. When the Word of God is not only preached with boldness but also lived with confidence, there is an atmosphere for change. There is a shift. We don't just hear truth . . . we live truth. As the Holy Spirit quickens us, we come to attention, stand straighter, and have a greater awareness that the truth we carry within us is sacred. When God's Word is preached through our lives, the Holy Spirit puts steel in our convictions. Those who have ears to hear will likewise receive the wisdom and courage to live in truth. The Word of God falls on good soil and produces a harvest first and foremost in our lives. This happens first in us so it can happen next through us.

Recently, I had a text conversation with the beautiful, young, brave daughter in the faith. She asked me how I reconciled the fact that public people with amazing spiritual gifts had personal lives that were in shambles. Their private lives were plagued with everything from adultery, alcohol abuse, to a lack of financial transparency. I explained that I believe our lives preach louder than our gifts. God's gifts are meant to be surrounded by the fruit of the Spirit, which is cultivated when we allow truth to have its way.

We know the truth, we cannot act as though we are ignorant of it. If we don't know the truth, we are invited to seek it. We seek it in God's Word and see it in the life of Jesus. And once it's discovered, we cannot continue to close our ears to the deafening cry for truth in a culture captive to the lies it told itself. Even now people are discovering that what they thought was freedom is in fact chains.

Jesus is our truth in a world of lies.

We adamantly oppose any degradation of the truth by living the Word of truth. Truth should be evident in our personal lives. We cannot choose to remain in a posture of quiet comfort when so many are living in the discomfort of lies.

Excerpted from Adamant *by Lisa Bevere. Copyright ©2018 by Lisa Bevere. Published by Revell, a division of Baker Publishing Group. Used by permission.*

SPIRIT . . .

When we accept Christ, we are given a new spirit. One of Christ's promises was that He left us with One like Him (see John 14:15–21). In other words, the Holy Spirit now dwells within us. And Scripture tells us that there are fruits of the Spirit that we can now see in our own lives!

But the fruit of the Spirit is love, joy, peace, longsuffering, kindness, goodness, faithfulness, gentleness, self-control. Against such there is no law (Galatians 5:22–23, NKJV).

PRAYER:

God, help us live with bold faith that we can experience the power of the resurrected Christ living within us. We have been offered forgiveness and the opportunity to live in fullness and fruitfulness for the rest of our lives. Jesus, You are the way. You are alive in us. Let us live with yielded hearts and minds, believing that Your will be done in and through us. Amen.

WORD OF ENCOURAGEMENT:

God promises to finish the work He starts in us (see Philippians 1:6).

God doesn't do things in half—

we can trust that He works things to their completion. When He begins something, we can have faith in His finished work. When He starts a work in us, He will be sure to complete it!

AND BECAUSE OF HIS GLORY
AND EXCELLENCE, HE HAS GIVEN US
GREAT AND PRECIOUS PROMISES.
THESE ARE THE PROMISES THAT
ENABLE YOU TO SHARE HIS DIVINE NATURE
AND ESCAPE THE WORLD'S CORRUPTION
CAUSED BY HUMAN DESIRES.

2 Peter 1:4 (NLT)

When we seek the Lord, we don't lack anything that we need. In fact, God promises that our needs will be met! This doesn't mean that we get everything that we want or even everything that we pray for, but we can trust that God will take care of us and provide for our needs.

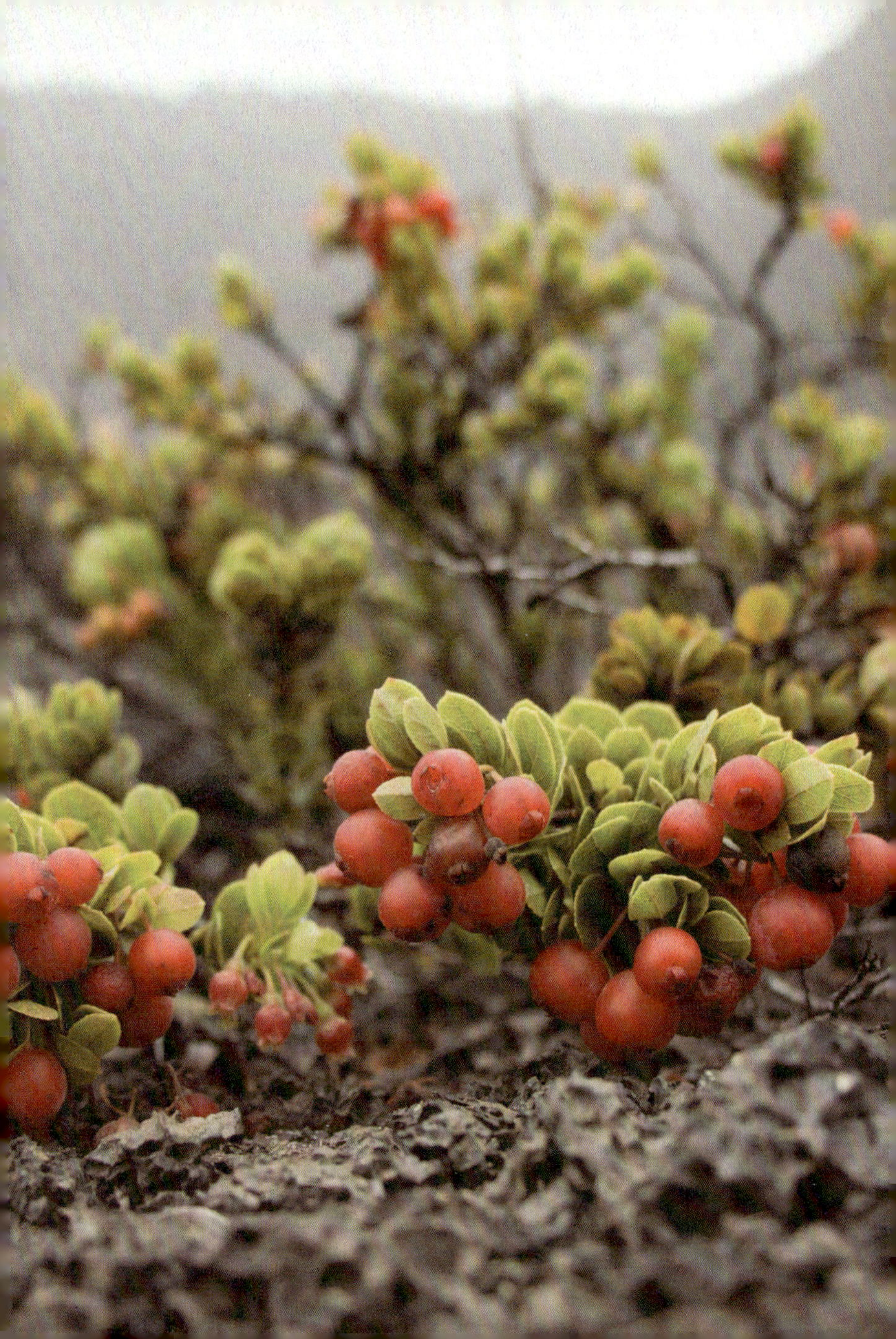

INSIGHT FOUR:

The Promise of the Prodigal

When trying to understand the heart of our Father, we see Him clearly revealed in the world-famous story known as "The Parable of the Prodigal Son."

In this story, Jesus tells of a father who had two sons. One of them went to his father, saying, "I want all of my inheritance, and I want it now!" The father, in love, permitted the son to have his share of the family inheritance. The rebellious lad went into a far country and wasted all his substance and wealth with riotous, selfish, self-centered, wicked living. When he had lost everything he had, he was actually forced to sell himself as a slave in that far country just to survive. The owner and master sent him into the pigpen to feed the hogs. While in the pigpen, he realized the sorry state that he had reached, how he in foolishness and rebellion had left the security and love of a relationship with his father and had gone out to have his own way in life.

All of us at some point have chosen to take all God has entrusted to us and have done our own thing.

Many have wasted their substance in this way. And please understand that every moment we live outside the will of God and a proper relationship with the Father is wasted. Believe it when I say the "far country" is one step outside the will of God. The problem has nothing to do with distance. It is simply the matter of our setting out to do our own thing, rather than seeking with all our heart to do the will of God. When we do that, we inevitably find that, as a result of our ways, we are sold out to some system of slavery in this world.

Thankfully, that's not the end of the story because God has promised us far more above and beyond our own sin. We all have the option to return to a Father who waits for us with open arms. And I can promise you that you will be blessed by His unconditional love and grace.

Who else has numbered
the very hairs on our head?
Who else observes every act
of our lives with a care so intense
that not even a sparrow can fall
to the ground without His notice?
Jesus pointed out that we are
of much greater value than
sparrows and assured us that
*if God watches over the birds
of the air and all created beings
and provides for them all,
He is surely much more certain
to watch over and provide for us.*

SEE MATTHEW 6:26–34

WORD OF ENCOURAGEMENT:

When we recognize that we have placed ourselves in bondage and fallen into the resulting pigpen of despair and defeat, we can do what the prodigal son correctly and wisely did; he got up and went back to the father.

When he neared his father's home, something truly remarkable happened. He didn't get the angry, scolding reception he probably expected and thought he deserved. His father was watching for him. I believe he looked every day to see if this boy might come down that road.

No matter how far we miss the mark or stray from home, **God is always watching for us, waiting patiently for our return.**

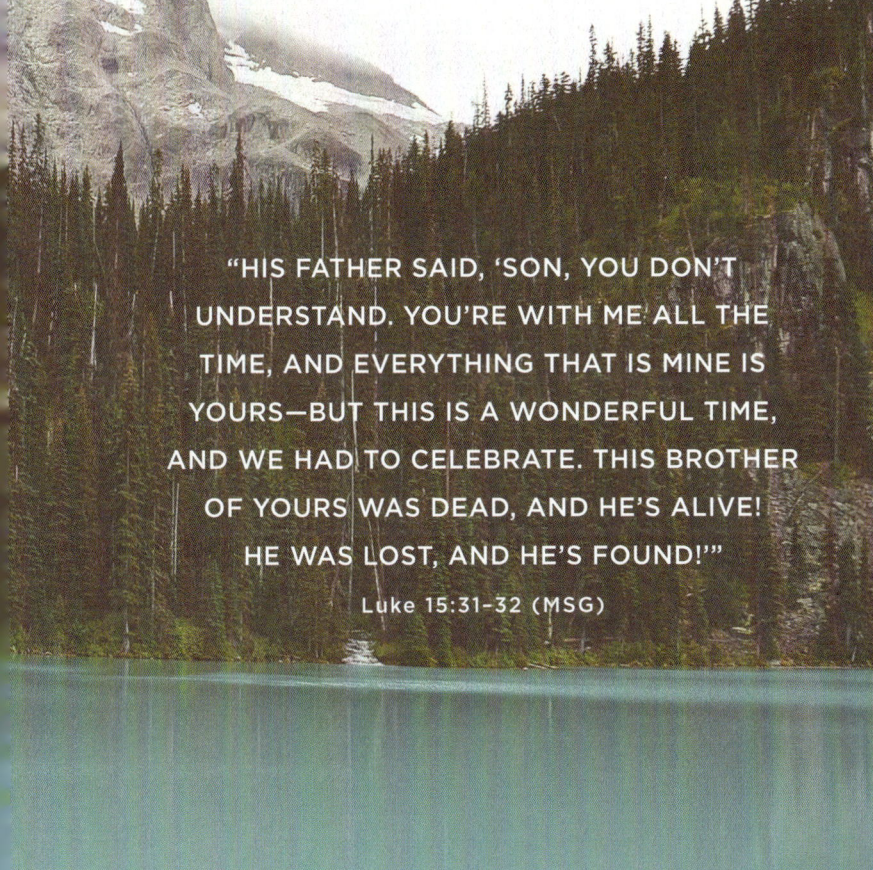

"HIS FATHER SAID, 'SON, YOU DON'T UNDERSTAND. YOU'RE WITH ME ALL THE TIME, AND EVERYTHING THAT IS MINE IS YOURS—BUT THIS IS A WONDERFUL TIME, AND WE HAD TO CELEBRATE. THIS BROTHER OF YOURS WAS DEAD, AND HE'S ALIVE! HE WAS LOST, AND HE'S FOUND!'"

Luke 15:31-32 (MSG)

STORY: JOHN ELDREDGE

I became a follower of Jesus at nineteen and knew God was our Father, but I lament that I have only sought his fathering in the past several years.

Most of us seek something to replace the demands of relationship. What we want right off the bat is a map of some kind, a plan, a clear path to begin walking down. Something that makes it clear what is important for us to do, and how to start doing it right now.

Nobody gets the master plan, not even a five-year overview—have you ever wondered why? The reason is simple and massively disruptive:

God wants us to seek him,

draw near to him, learn to walk with him, and frankly we won't do it if we have a plan to follow instead.

And so we come to the heart of so many problems. . . . We don't find fulfillment because that can only be satisfied by the One who created us and predestined our purpose. Discovering that purpose begins with a simple concept:

repentance, which simply means to turn around.

It begins with posture...

I need a father; I have a father; I am going to seek my father. Isn't that the turning point in the story of the prodigal son? He shook off his independence and took on a new posture, a willingness to turn father-ward... and it saved him.

Excerpted from Killing Lions *by John and Sam Eldredge. Copyright ©2014 by John and Sam Eldredge. Published by Nelson Books, an imprint of Thomas Nelson, Inc. All rights reserved.*

HOUSE ...

When we are with God, we are truly at home. The most comfortable, natural position is to be in the company of our Father. Jesus assures us of this in the gospel of John:

"Do not let your heart be troubled ... In my Father's house are many dwelling places; if it were not so, I would have told you; for I go to prepare a place for you" (John 14:1–2, NASB).

Jesus has gone ahead of us to prepare our heavenly house. This is a promise we can look forward to!

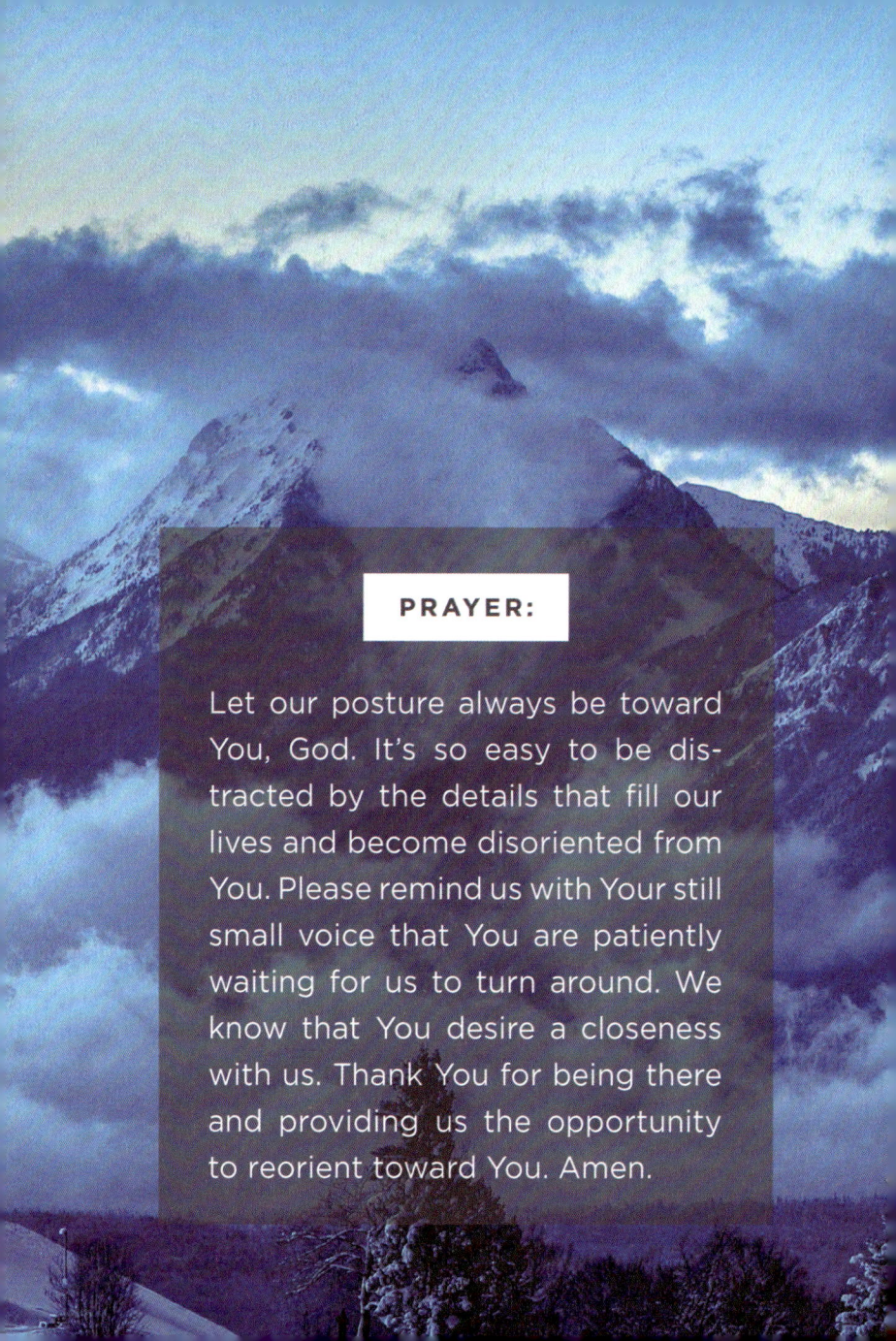

PRAYER:

Let our posture always be toward You, God. It's so easy to be distracted by the details that fill our lives and become disoriented from You. Please remind us with Your still small voice that You are patiently waiting for us to turn around. We know that You desire a closeness with us. Thank You for being there and providing us the opportunity to reorient toward You. Amen.

WORD OF ENCOURAGEMENT:

It's so comforting to me that Jesus refers to Himself as the Good Shepherd. Do you know it is not the sheep's job to get themselves home? So often we worry about this in our lives. We're so preoccupied with getting it right. It's the shepherd's job, though. The shepherd always goes ahead of the sheep and leads them home. It is our job to stay close to His heart **and He will get us home.**

Excerpted from LIFE TODAY *taping with Sheila Walsh, May 3, 2011.*

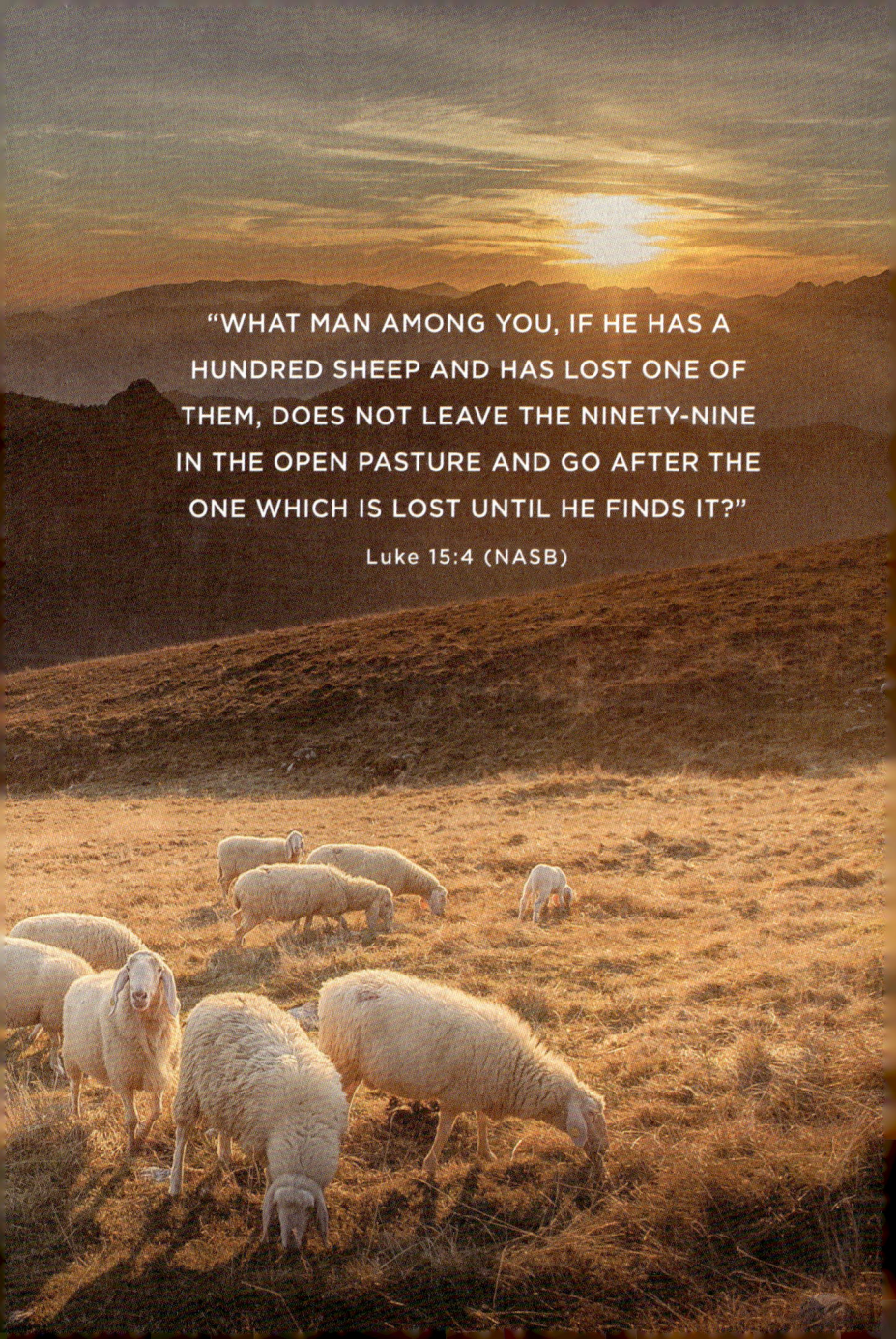

"WHAT MAN AMONG YOU, IF HE HAS A HUNDRED SHEEP AND HAS LOST ONE OF THEM, DOES NOT LEAVE THE NINETY-NINE IN THE OPEN PASTURE AND GO AFTER THE ONE WHICH IS LOST UNTIL HE FINDS IT?"

Luke 15:4 (NASB)

STORY: JAMES ROBISION

My father had no desire whatsoever to be part of my life. He never took me fishing. He never played ball with me. He never said, "That's good, son." His lack of involvement deeply wounded me and created a terrible sense of insecurity, guilt and fear – feelings that handicapped me emotionally for many years. It was only when I met Jesus, and He introduced me to His perfect, Heavenly Father, that I was able to overcome the hurts of the past and find real meaning in life. Regardless of our background, circumstances, failures or successes, each of us has a deep and very real personal need for a relationship with God as Father. He is the one and only perfect Father . . .

He is the all-knowing, all-caring, all-sufficient, almighty God.

Yet in His written Word, the Bible, God reveals Himself to us as our Father.

What an incredible blessing to have God reveal Himself as our Father. Not just any father, but a Father who loves unconditionally, intercedes on our behalf, blesses us immeasurably and so much more.

And regardless of sin, our Heavenly Father keeps His arms wide open for us like the prodigal son's father.

Jesus told this parable as a reminder to us of His vast love and deep care. When the father finally saw his son coming down the road, he didn't look the same as he did when he left.

Then he was haughty and arrogant, proud and standing tall. Now, coming down the dusty road, he was the figure of one stooped, bent and broken. But the father knew him. It was his boy!

And I can promise you, the minute you turn your heart toward God and head toward your wonderful, loving Heavenly Father, He will do more than meet you halfway. He will run as that boy's father did to receive you in His arms.

LOVE...

As a child of God, your Father loves you immeasurably. It's a love that is hard to comprehend—a love so great that He sent Jesus to die for us. We have affirmation of this promise in 1 John 3:1:

See how great a love the Father has bestowed on us, that we would be called children of God... (NASB).

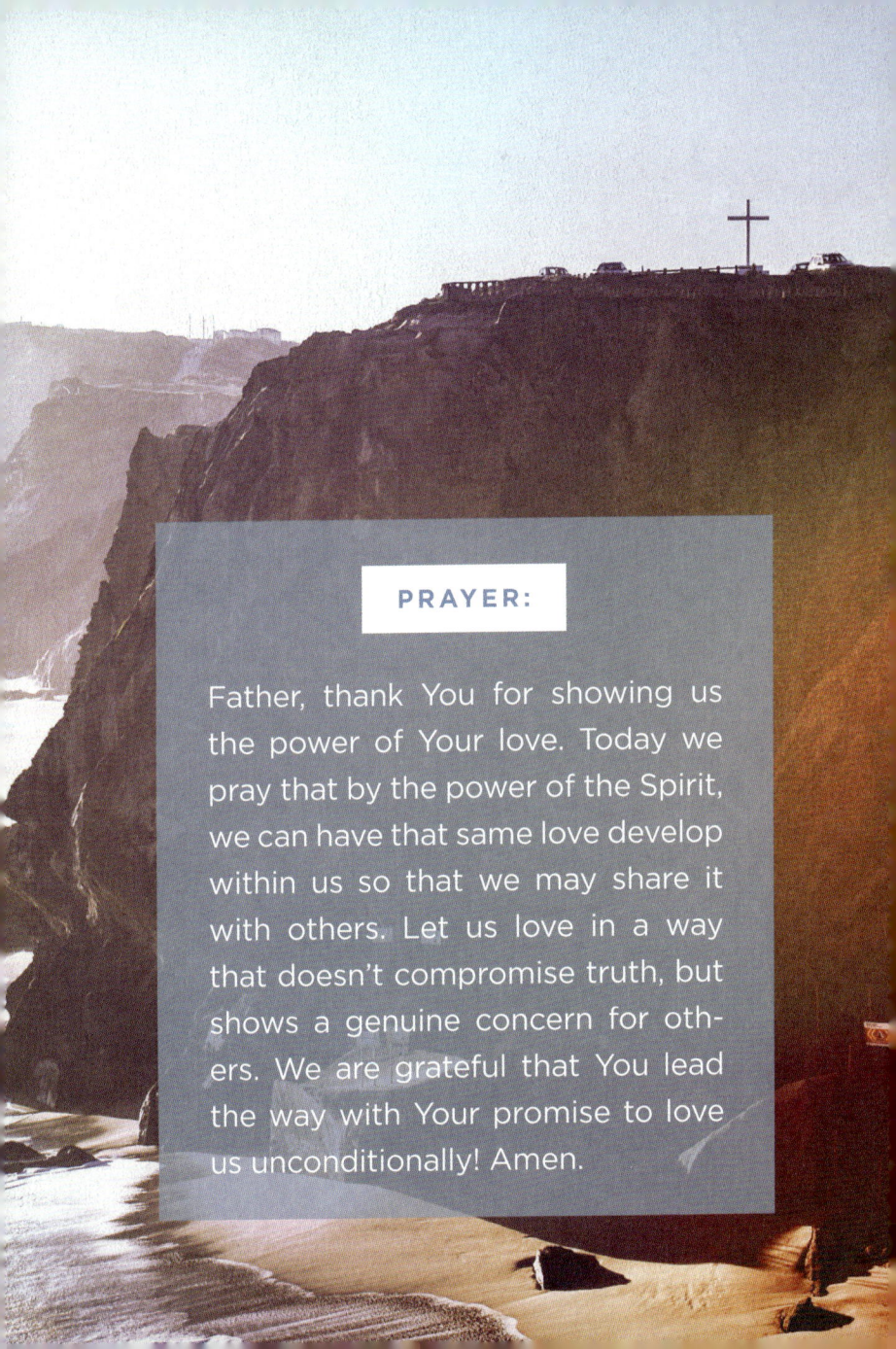

PRAYER:

Father, thank You for showing us the power of Your love. Today we pray that by the power of the Spirit, we can have that same love develop within us so that we may share it with others. Let us love in a way that doesn't compromise truth, but shows a genuine concern for others. We are grateful that You lead the way with Your promise to love us unconditionally! Amen.

WORD OF ENCOURAGEMENT:

With God as our Father, He does for us the things we can't do for ourselves. And, as we yield to Him and let Him renew and strengthen us, **He reveals what we are capable of doing through faith in Him!**

FOR GOD IS WORKING IN YOU,
GIVING YOU THE DESIRE
AND THE POWER TO
DO WHAT PLEASES HIM.

Philippians 2:13 (NLT)

He's the One who can
take the broken pieces
of any life and
work them together
like a puzzle that shapes
a beautiful masterpiece,
a portrait of joy,
peace and meaning.
That's what God wants
to do for you and
your loved ones.

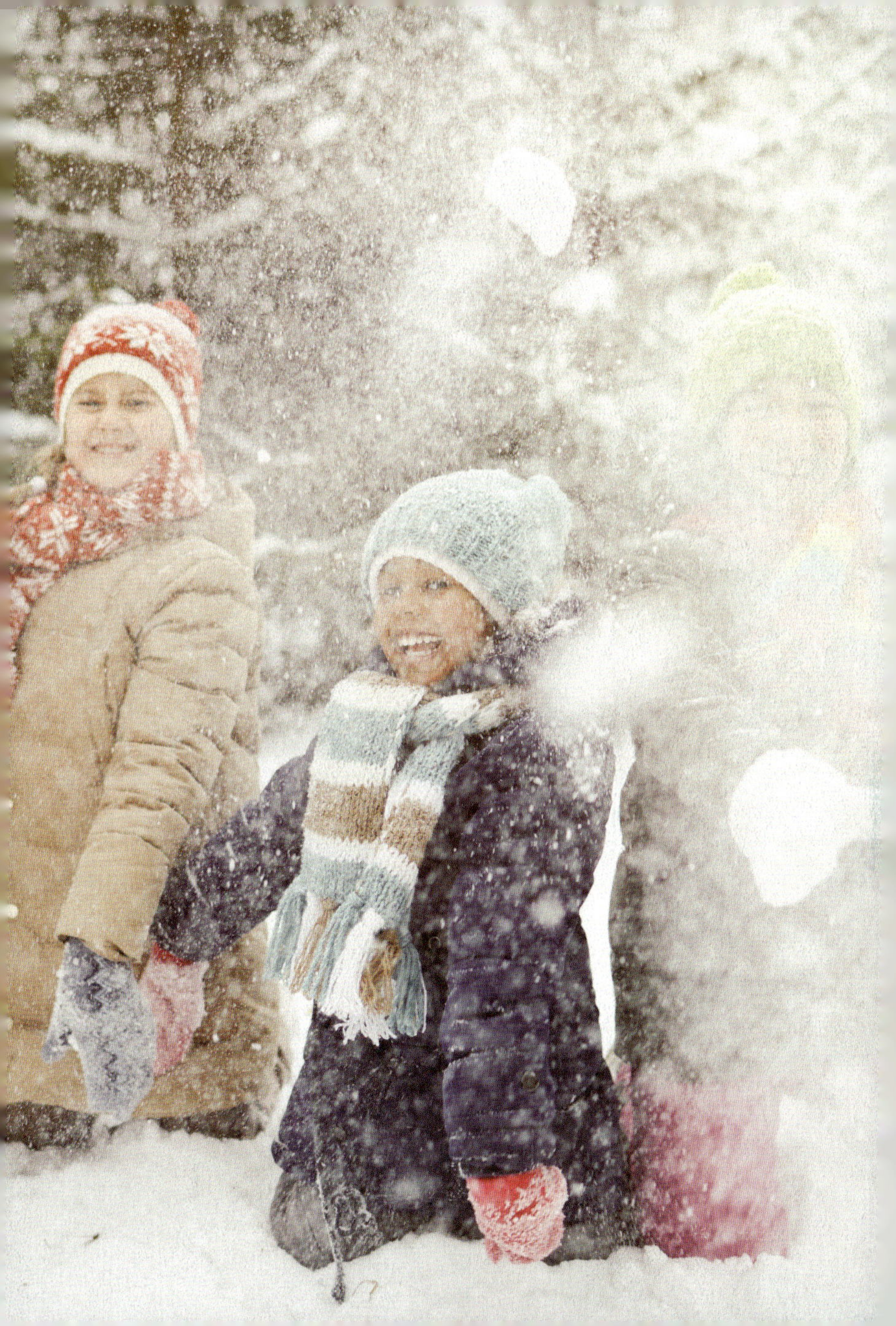

INSIGHT FIVE:

THE PROMISE OF PROTECTION

Everyone experiences unexpected problems. Some of your circumstances may seem to have gone haywire. You may have run into opposition from people you thought were on your side. You might be facing physical, emotional or spiritual issues even as you read this. In other words, you may feel that you have been attacked.

If this sort of thing is happening to you, ***don't be alarmed or discouraged***. And if they are not happening, don't be smug—because sooner or later they will come upon you.

When you become a child of God, you become involved in a spiritual battle. Jesus warned us that those who hate Him will hate us (see John 15:18–19).

But God promises in Isaiah 54:17 that we are protected.

"No weapon formed against you shall prosper, and every tongue which rises against you in judgment you shall condemn. This is the heritage of the servants of the LORD, and their righteousness is from Me," says the LORD (NKJV).

Our Father is committed to be our Protector in every circumstance that may come against us. No matter what spiritual battle you may feel you are in, trust in His promise that He will protect you.

Sometimes God's protection comes in the form of deliverance. In the spiritual wars you face daily, the enemy sets all kinds of traps for you. They may take the form of addictions, destructive patterns of thought and behavior, scheming people or the unseen agents and powers of darkness. But whatever they are, your Father promises to deliver you and protect you.

At other times, God's protection may look more like a refuge. In the midst of a storm, you can always seek Him and be assured that you will find calmness in His Word and His presence. And even still, sometimes God's protection is simply miraculous. He continues to work in ways that we don't always understand; and when these moments arise, we just give thanks for His promise of protection.

As you walk confidently in the promise of deliverance, remember your position as a child of God. Trust Him in every situation for deliverance, whether it comes immediately, incrementally or eternally. And most importantly, always know that our deliverance lies in staying close to the One who is our Deliverer.

— RANDY ROBISON

WORD OF ENCOURAGEMENT:

I went through one of the greatest crises of my life in 2018. I found out my 20-year-old son had cancer, and it was a very life-threatening cancer. The Lord really worked miracles, and my son had an incredible healing. The day after I found out, though, I was weeping. The Lord said, "Open your book." I opened it to a page with everything Jesus said on anxiety, worry and fear.

When we get in trouble, we run to our relatives, we run to our friends, we run to counselors, but we don't run to Christ. He says, "Come to me first. Learn from me." He has answered everything!

Excerpted from LIFE TODAY *taping with Steve Scott, November 13, 2014.*

I LOOK UP TO THE MOUNTAINS—
DOES MY HELP COME FROM THERE?
MY HELP COMES FROM THE LORD,
WHO MADE HEAVEN AND EARTH!

HE WILL NOT LET YOU STUMBLE;
THE ONE WHO WATCHES OVER YOU WILL
NOT SLUMBER. INDEED, HE WHO WATCHES
OVER ISRAEL NEVER SLUMBERS OR SLEEPS.

THE LORD HIMSELF WATCHES OVER YOU!
THE LORD STANDS BESIDE YOU AS YOUR
PROTECTIVE SHADE. THE SUN WILL NOT
HARM YOU BY DAY, NOR THE MOON AT NIGHT.

THE LORD KEEPS YOU FROM ALL HARM AND
WATCHES OVER YOUR LIFE. THE LORD KEEPS
WATCH OVER YOU AS YOU COME AND GO,
BOTH NOW AND FOREVER.

Psalm 121 (NLT)

GUEST: LYSA TERKEURST

We need to remember the difference between news and truth. News comes at us to tell us what we are dealing with. Truth comes from God and then helps us process all we are dealing with. News and truth aren't always one and the same.

My sweet friend Shaunti Feldhahn reminded me of this a few years ago. An e-mail she sent me about a difficulty I was walking through said, "Lysa, this is news. This is not truth."

What the doctor gave me was news. Honest news based on test results and medical facts. But what I have access to is a truth that transcends news. The restoration that is impossible with man's limitations is always possible for a limitless God. Truth is what factors God into the equation.

I find myself looking at the word *impossible* a little differently today.

Impossible, when looked at in light of Shaunti's note, could be completely different if I just stuck a little apostrophe between the first two letters. Then it becomes I'm-Possible. God is the great I AM.

Therefore, he is my possibility for hope and healing.

I'm-Possible is a much more comforting way to look at anything that feels quite impossible—anything that feels like it's too much for me to handle. Instead of saying God won't give me more than I can handle, maybe I can just simply say,

"God's got a handle on all I'm facing."

Excerpted from It's Not Supposed To Be This Way *by Lysa TerKeurst. Copyright ©2018 by Lysa TerKeurst. Used by permission of Nelson Books, an imprint of Thomas Nelson.*

DELIVER...

When we call upon Christ as our power and strength, He promises to deliver us from spiritual attacks. So many things in this world can bind us... whether it's an addiction, a harmful thought pattern or behavior, an unhealthy relationship, finances or any other force.

Remember to call on Christ as your Deliverer! He reaches down to pull you out of the deepest, darkest pits into His love and light.

PRAYER:

Lord, I know that You will protect me. You have the power and strength and sovereignty needed to deliver me from any spiritual darkness that attempts to take hold of me. But in Your name, it will not overpower me. You are my Protector, my Deliverer, my Rock. Thank you, Jesus. Amen.

WORD OF ENCOURAGEMENT:

You may face problems and challenges that you feel you don't have the strength to handle. You simply won't be able to deal with them in your human ability. It may be the death of a close loved one. Or a severe physical illness or disability. Or a betrayal by someone you completely trusted. Or a disastrous setback in your career or finances. Such ordeals are never pleasant for us at the time. When you became God's child, you became a being possessing supernatural strength. **Your Father earnestly desires that you know the strength you have in Him!**

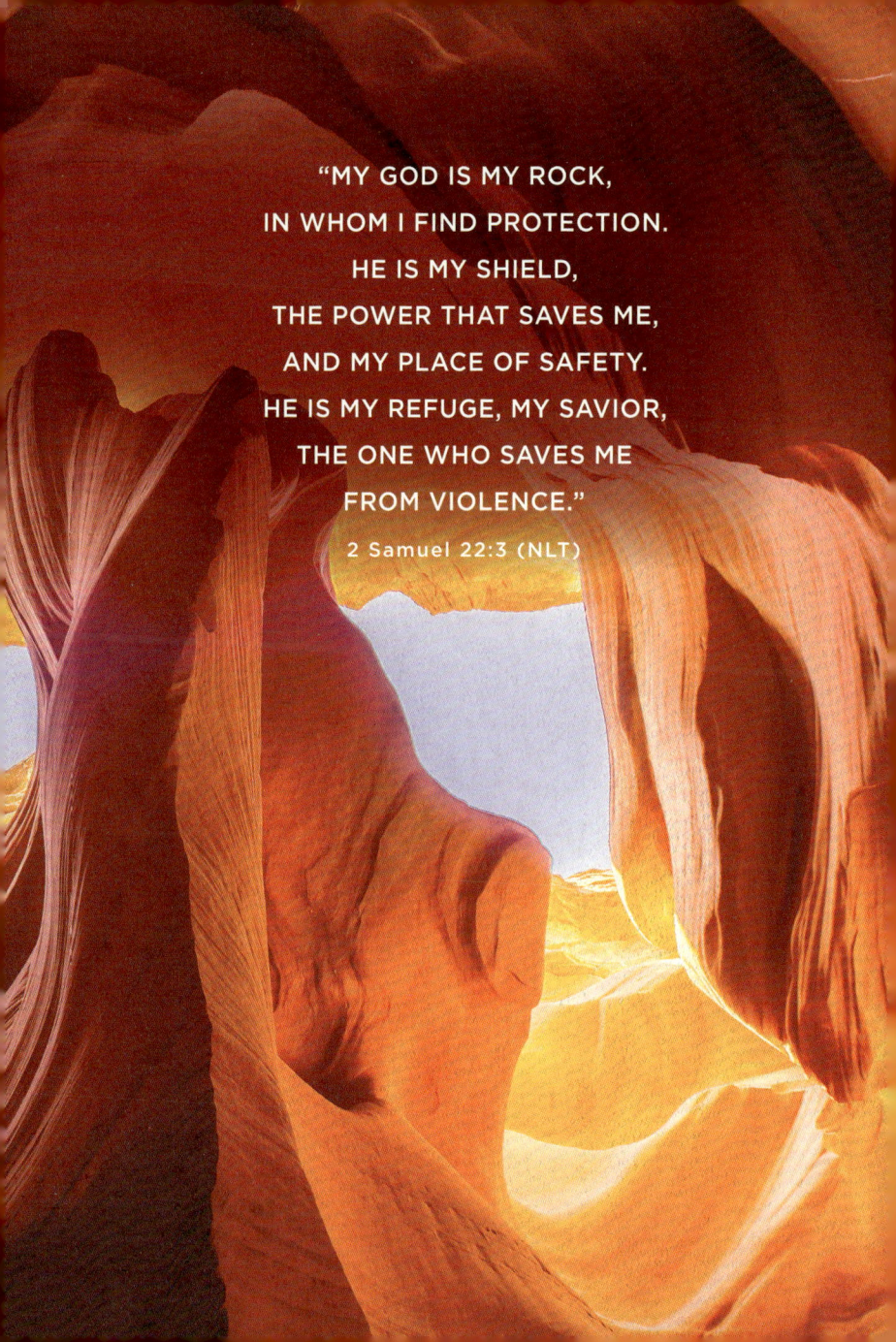

"MY GOD IS MY ROCK,
IN WHOM I FIND PROTECTION.
HE IS MY SHIELD,
THE POWER THAT SAVES ME,
AND MY PLACE OF SAFETY.
HE IS MY REFUGE, MY SAVIOR,
THE ONE WHO SAVES ME
FROM VIOLENCE."

2 Samuel 22:3 (NLT)

STORY: PETER PRETORIUS

For the next couple of years, we often drove back and forth from our home in Nelspruit to Maputo and other points in Mozambique. Every time we reached the border I'd have to fight the fear that engulfed me because of the impending dangers I could face during the next few hours. I knew that as soon as I crossed that imaginary line, my life was at risk.

We continued to encounter burned-out shells of cars and trucks. Some were still burning or smoldering. We also continued to encounter other obstacles, including numerous military roadblocks. The worst thing about those roadblocks was that you never knew who was in charge. Were they government soldiers or rebels? It didn't matter that much because either side could be dangerous. . . . It was a time of intense pressure and real, heart-thumping, stomach-clinching fear. We had no option but to completely trust in God to get us safely through. . . .

We knew that God was with us.

[One day as I drove a stretch of road], I thought I saw something move. It was a couple of hundred meters in front of me, high up on the right side. I held my breath and squinted to get a better look. There it was again. As I drew closer, I could see that a rebel soldier was looking down on the roadway. The sun glinted off the barrel of his assault rifle.

. . . I didn't know what to do. I couldn't outrun a bullet. Once again, I called out the same name I had shouted on that racetrack so many years ago. "Jesus!" But this time it was a heartfelt prayer. "Please help me!"

Ahead of me, I saw the soldier exit the brush and stand on the roadside. He lifted his rifle and prepared to shoot. I tensed, awaiting the bullet that would end my life here on earth. It never came.

To this day, I don't know what happened. Perhaps his gun jammed, perhaps he changed his mind. Perhaps he was out of ammunition. All I know for sure is that I wasn't about to go back and ask him. Jesus heard my prayer and protected me once again as I took that curve.

Excerpted from Death-Defying Faith *by Peter Pretorius. Copyright © 2018 by Inprov, Ltd. Used by permission.*

STRENGTH...

God promises that He provides us with strength (see Philippians 4:13). We can call on this promise in every moment of weakness and trust that He holds us up, empowering us with a heavenly strength that enables us to overcome challenges. We can do everything through
Christ because He is our strength!

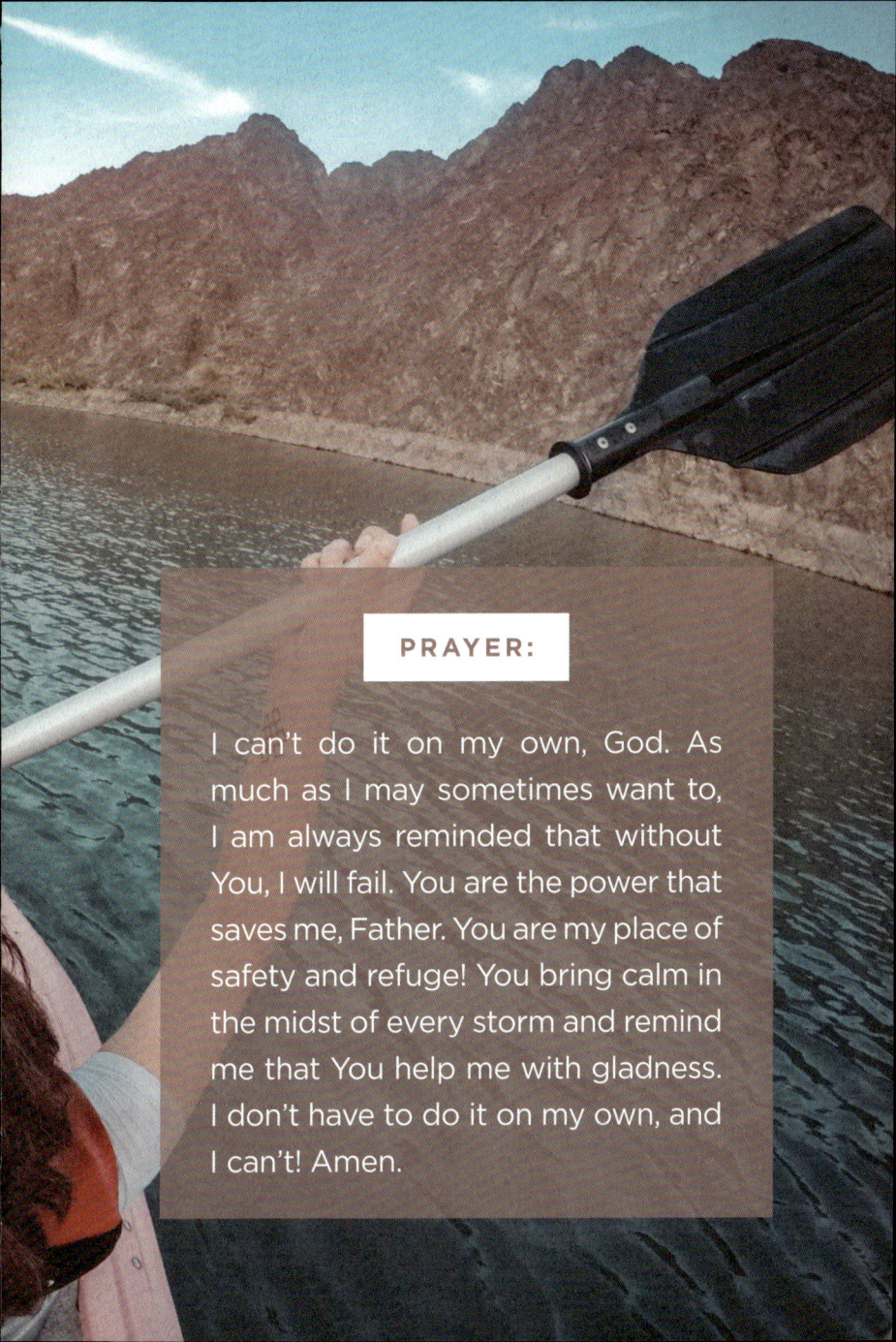

PRAYER:

I can't do it on my own, God. As much as I may sometimes want to, I am always reminded that without You, I will fail. You are the power that saves me, Father. You are my place of safety and refuge! You bring calm in the midst of every storm and remind me that You help me with gladness. I don't have to do it on my own, and I can't! Amen.

WORD OF ENCOURAGEMENT:

Father, let us not forget all the ways You protect and strengthen us. Help us to remember to simply **call on Your name when we face any trouble** or tribulation. You deliver us, You uphold us, You embolden us, You encourage us. Thank You!

GOD'S WAY IS PERFECT.
ALL THE LORD'S PROMISES
PROVE TRUE. HE IS A SHIELD
FOR ALL WHO LOOK TO HIM
FOR PROTECTION. FOR WHO IS GOD
EXCEPT THE LORD? WHO BUT OUR GOD
IS A SOLID ROCK? GOD ARMS ME WITH
STRENGTH, AND HE MAKES MY WAY PERFECT.

Psalm 18:30-32 (NLT)

What an encouragement to be able to read the Bible and see all the ways that God protects us. He is a refuge for us and a sure place to receive heavenly protection.

He is a fortress.
PSALM 18:2

He is a strong tower.
PROVERBS 18:10

He is a rock.
1 SAMUEL 2:2

He is our strength and protection.
PSALM 31:4

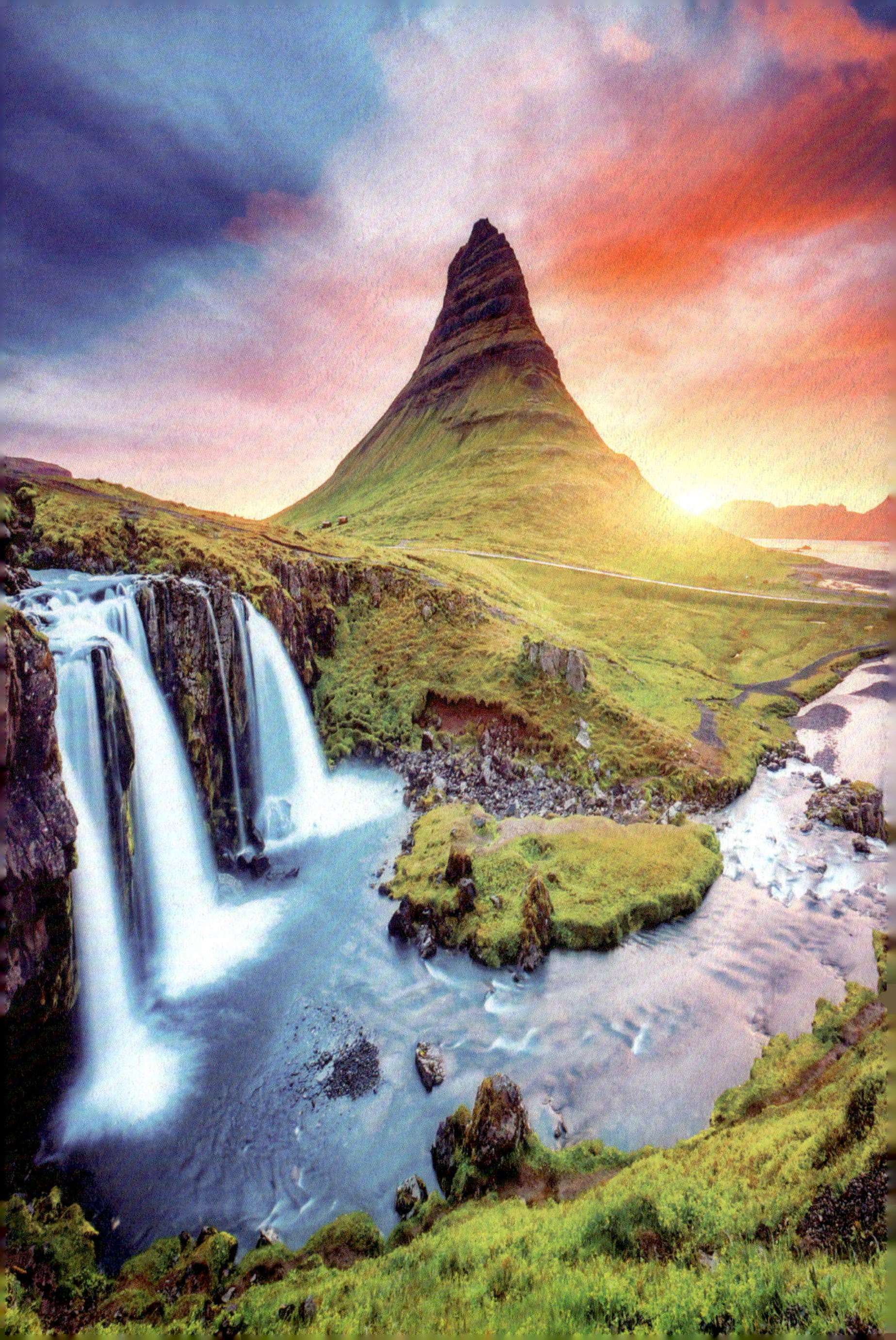

INSIGHT SIX:

THE PROMISE OF PEACE

In a world full of stress, anxiety, worry, fear and so many other powers of darkness, it can be hard to truly feel at peace. We try to get away for a weekend or take a vacation, but sometimes even that doesn't leave us feeling relaxed or refreshed. Why does it seem so difficult to find peace?

It turns out that peace isn't all that difficult to find after all, though. When we fix our eyes on Jesus and His promises for us and our lives, we will find that peace is with us even now.

The Bible is full of words of peace. We are promised that we receive the supernatural peace of God through Christ. The Kingdom of God is one of peace, love and righteousness. God gives us peace in the midst of every storm.

Not only do we have promises of peace from Christ, but Scripture tells us that Christ Himself is our peace (see Ephesians 2:14). We can count on Him as our place of refuge, and when we turn to Him in the midst of any anxiety, fear or worry, His peace transcends whatever we may be feeling or facing.

His Word also tells us that peace can sanctify us (see 1 Thessalonians 5:23). His peace multiplied in our lives brings a sense of supernatural calm in its purest form.

In Isaiah 53, we are even told that part of Christ's sacrifice was so that we could have peace; . . .*The chastisement for our peace was upon Him, and by His stripes we are healed* (Isaiah 53:5, NKJV).

I pray that every person in the body of Christ

can experience the true supernatural peace that can come only through Him. I pray that as you read of His peace, that you feel it wash over you.

And my hope for you is that it isn't a one-time experience, but rather His peace stays with you for all your days.

You can live a life with the promised peace of God within your heart,

extending the grace and charity of Christ to all you encounter.

At some point, you have probably thought of God as a Being who lived far away from you. Even many Christians, years after being born again, feel there is a great distance between them and their Heavenly Father. But this is not true. God has welcomed us into His very presence through Jesus. He has made us His dwelling place through His Holy Spirit, who lives in us. There is an overwhelming sense of peace when we realize just how close He really is!

WORD OF ENCOURAGEMENT:

A lot of people are hurting right now. I mean hurting tremendously. But the people who really put God first in their life have a peace and confidence that

God is going to take care of me

[them] even if I go through some difficulty.

Excerpted from LIFE TODAY *taping with Robert Morris, 12/27/11.*

"THESE THINGS I HAVE SPOKEN TO YOU, THAT IN ME YOU MAY HAVE PEACE. . . ."

John 16:33 (NKJV)

TESTIMONY: BETTY ROBISON

When James and I found deliverance from the strongholds in our lives, we still had to learn the importance of standing together against Satan's schemes, because when God removed those strongholds, there was an empty place that had to be filled with something.

When God released me from the spirit of fear that had governed my life for so long, I had to fill that empty room to keep the tormentors from coming back. I had to learn how to relate to people apart from fear, and it didn't just naturally happen.

God gave me supernatural help,

filling my life—His temple—with love, peace, and joy, along with a sound mind in place of that overwhelming fear.
I now have a sense of freedom, knowing that God had removed the spirit of fear, but I couldn't say, "Okay, I'm fixed. It's all over. I don't have to deal with that anymore." I still had to allow God to bring healing to

my heart, to teach me how to resist fear, and to make me strong enough to stand against the enemy's attacks.

As with Jesus during His temptation by Satan, the enemy looks for every opportune moment to attack us. James and I are determined to fill the house that God cleansed with the truth of His Word and to daily build up and renew our hearts and minds.

One important change that came about as a result of my deliverance was that I learned to depend on God rather than James for my sense of worth and security. Because James was my husband and because of the evident work of the Spirit in his life, I had placed James on a pedestal. I expected him to come through for me whenever I had a need, but God let me know that He, not my husband, was to be my first love and my deliverer. When I allowed Jesus to be the rightful head of our home, James was freed to take his place as my companion and friend.

Excerpted from Living In Love *by permission of WaterBrook Press, a division of Penguin Random House, LLC.*
Copyright ©2010 by Betty Robison. All rights reserved.

UNDERSTANDING...

Not only has God promised us peace, but He has promised us a peace that transcends our understanding. There is so much about our Father that can be difficult to comprehend. He is all-powerful and all-knowing. He is the beginning and the end, outside of time. Yet, even when we can't understand just how great His love is, we know that He gives us a peace that guards our hearts and minds (see Philippians 4:7).

PRAYER:

Lord, help us remember that we need not be anxious or worry about anything. Instead, through faith, we know that we can always come to You in prayer. I can talk to You all day long, Father, and You listen! You grant me a peace that overcomes all anxiety and fear; and the moment I call on Your name, I feel that peace wash over me. Amen.

WORD OF ENCOURAGEMENT:

You may wonder, *How can I ever have peace in light of everything I am going through?* The strife in the world, your conflicts with others, and the stresses of life make gaining real peace seem impossible. But God says to us, "Child, I want to give you a peace that the world cannot give or even understand. This peace can be found only in Me, and it passes all human understanding. To receive it, you need to believe in Me to the point of daily abiding in My words and doing them. This will bring you into intimacy with the Father and Me. This peace is so fulfilling that those who have it can joyfully endure any hardship or trial. When you are stressed, worried, or fearful, let that be an alarm warning you that you have taken your eyes off Me. You have stopped trusting Me, and you are no longer abiding in My words and acting on them. Reset your focus and run to My words.

Then *rest* in Me."

Copyright ©2015 by Steven K. Scott. Excerpted from Jesus Speaks *by permission of WaterBrook Press, a division of Penguin Random House, LLC. All rights reserved.*

PEACE I LEAVE WITH YOU;
MY PEACE I GIVE TO YOU;
NOT AS THE WORLD GIVES
DO I GIVE TO YOU. DO NOT
LET YOUR HEART BE TROUBLED,
NOR LET IT BE FEARFUL.

John 14:27 (NASB)

STORY: MARK BATTERSON

In July 2016, I kicked off a series of sermons at our church called *Mountains Move,* and I just felt this stirring to challenge our church to pray the bravest prayer. What I mean by that, is a prayer that just seems so impossible, or maybe a prayer that you've prayed 100 times and God hasn't answered it.

I said to our church, "For me, the bravest prayer is that the Lord would heal my asthma." Now the reason why I say that is because my earliest memory is an asthma attack. Probably three, four years old, I end up in the emergency room and that happened night after night. Over 40 years and there weren't 40 days that I didn't take an inhaler. I've been Code Blue, I've been in the intensive care unit a dozen times. For whatever reason the Lord just did not answer that prayer until that day in July 2016.

Pray that prayer one more time . . .

Let's not make this all neat and clean. Like even Jesus when he heals the man who is blind, he does it twice, right? Sometimes it is a process. And sometimes I've found, you almost have to take that first little step of faith. So it just became evident to me that something has shifted, something has changed.

I heard God whisper to me as a teenager, "Mark, I just want you to know that I am able." I held onto that whisper all these years. Hold onto those whispers.

Excerpted from LIFE TODAY *taping with Mark Batterson, 10/16/17.*

COVENANT . . .

In Isaiah, God promised that both His unfailing love and covenant of peace would always be with us (see Isaiah 54:10). Our Lord has compassion for us, a tender heart for His children; and no matter what happens, His promises remain. Even if the mountains shake or the hills move, we will still have His peace!

PRAYER:

Father, in the book of Isaiah, You promised us perfect peace. When our minds are on You, we receive a heavenly peace that can transcend all worry, anxiety, fear or doubt. Today we pray to meditate on this promise, remembering that You are the source of perfect peace! Thank You for Your power over any anxiety, fear or worry that we may be feeling. Amen.

WORD OF ENCOURAGEMENT:

The peace we receive from God is a peace that we cannot receive from the world. We know that every good and perfect gift comes from above, and Christ's promise of peace is no exception. In fact, He is referred to as the Prince of Peace in the Bible! What better peace could we be given than that which is given straight from the Prince of Peace?

FOR TO US A CHILD IS BORN,
TO US A SON IS GIVEN;
AND THE GOVERNMENT
SHALL BE UPON HIS SHOULDER,
AND HIS NAME SHALL BE CALLED
WONDERFUL COUNSELOR, MIGHTY GOD,
EVERLASTING FATHER, PRINCE OF PEACE.

Isaiah 9:6 (ESV)

FATHER,

THANK YOU FOR YOUR PROMISES. YOUR WORD DOES NOT FAIL! YOU GIVE US SO MUCH—YOUR LOVE, YOUR PEACE, YOUR PROTECTION, YOUR WISDOM, YOUR GUIDANCE, YOUR GRACE. WE ARE CONSTANTLY RECEIVING FROM YOU ALL THESE THINGS THAT WE WILL NEVER BE DESERVING OF. WE KNOW THAT YOU HAVE A SPIRITUAL INHERITANCE FOR US THAT IS ABOVE AND BEYOND ANYTHING WE COULD EVER DREAM OF.

AMEN.

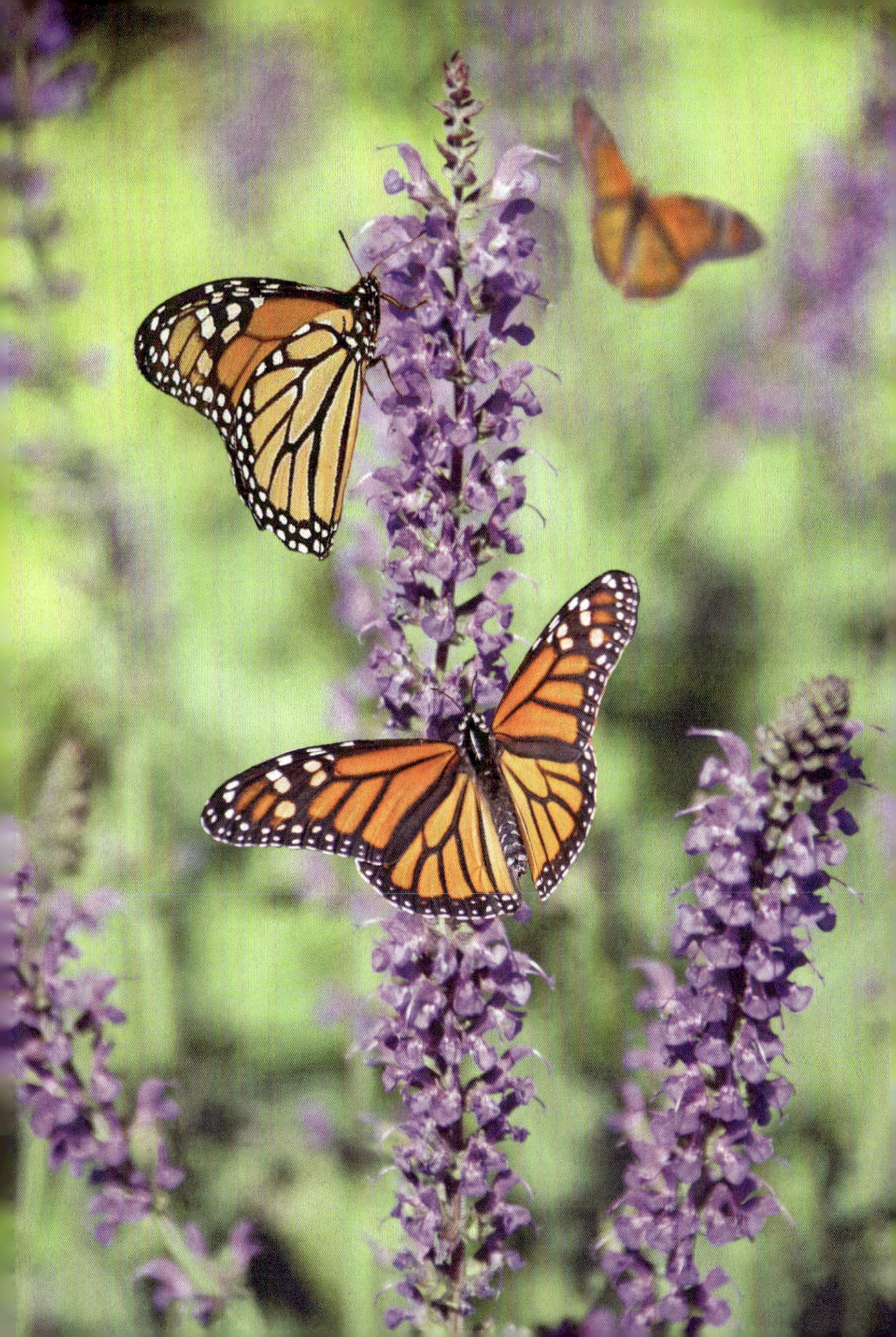

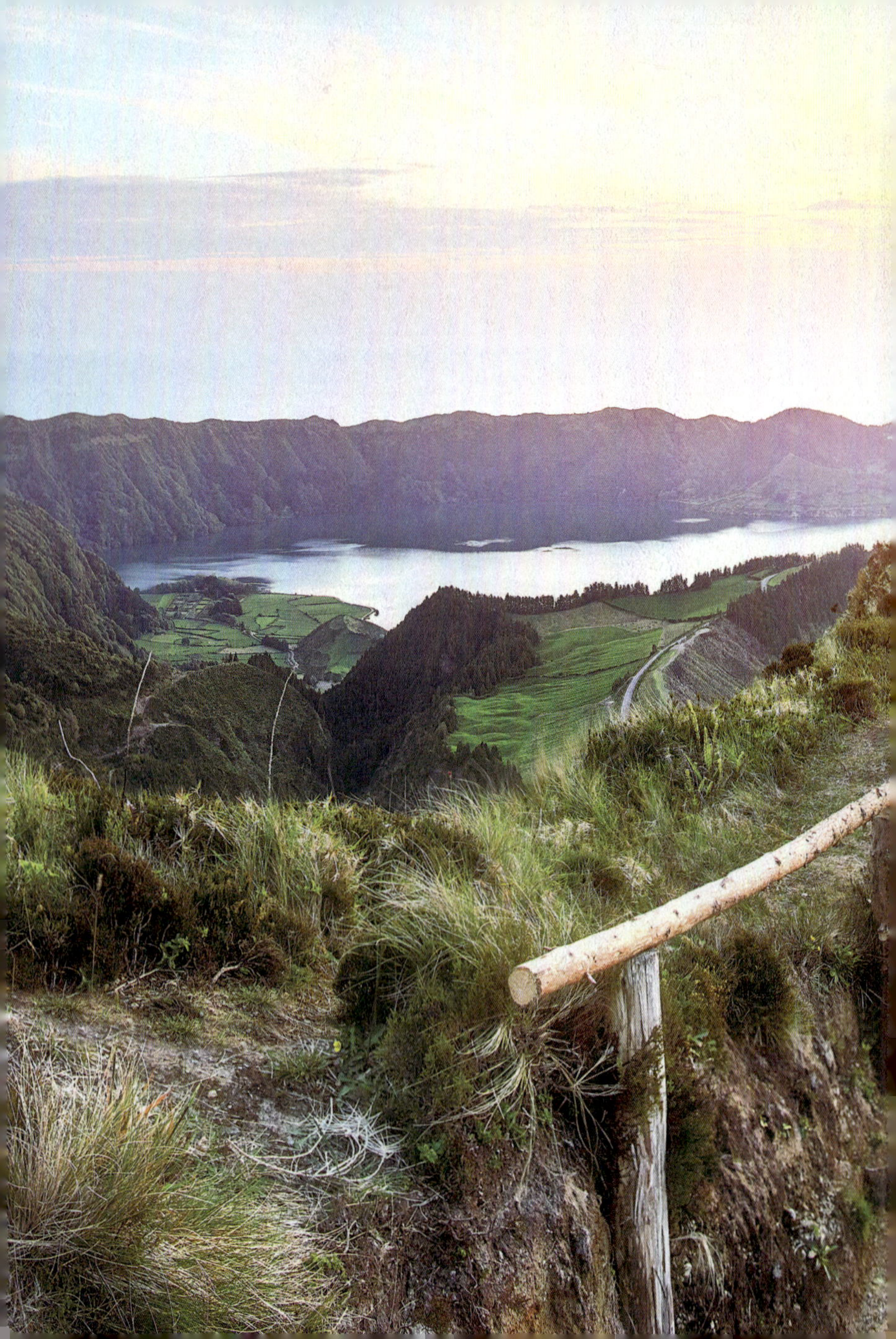

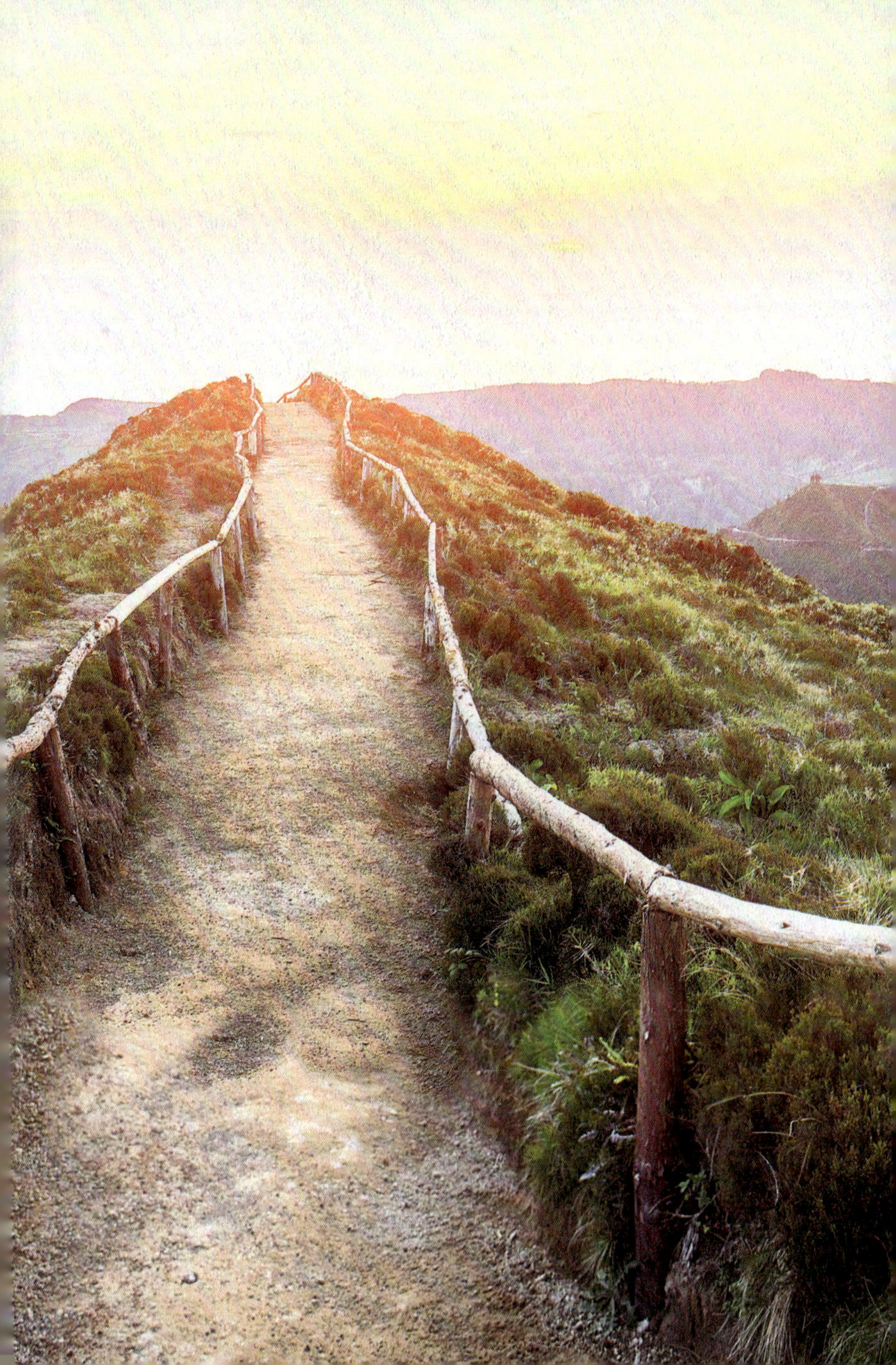